W9-ASI-633

ERRATA

Please note the following corrections in Chapter 3 (pp. 44-54), "National Crime Surveys: Victim Reports":

Figures 3.1 and 3.2 are reversed in the text. Figure 3.1 should appear on page 44; 3.2 should appear on page 53.

Thirteen lines of text that were printed on page 53 should be moved to the top of page 45. Thus, the sentence that begins at the bottom of page 43 should read as follows:

For example, "if a robber enters a bar and robs the cash register receipts and a wallet from the bartender and personal property from five patrons, the *UCR* counts only one robbery; there was a single incident of robbery in which there were six victimizations" (Garofalo and Hindelang, 1977: 22).

Robert M. O'Brien, *Crime and Victimization Data* (Law and Criminal Justice Series, Volume 4).

Crime
and
Victimization
Data

LAW AND CRIMINAL JUSTICE SERIES

Series Editor: James A. Inciardi
Division of Criminal Justice, University of Delaware

The **Law and Criminal Justice Series** provides students in criminal justice, criminology, law, sociology, and related fields with a set of short textbooks on major topics and subareas of the field. The texts range from books that introduce the basic elements of criminal justice for lower division undergraduates to more advanced topics of current interest for advanced undergraduates and beginning graduate students. Each text is concise, didactic, and produced in an inexpensive paperback as well as hardcover format. Each author addresses the major issues and areas of current concern in that topic area, reporting on and synthesizing major research done on the subject. Case examples, chapter summaries, and discussion questions are generally included in each volume to aid in classroom usage. The module format of the series provides an attractive alternative to large, expensive classroom textbooks or timely supplements to more traditional class materials.

Volumes in this series:

1: THE AMERICAN SYSTEM OF CRIMINAL JUSTICE,
   Geoffrey P. Alpert
2: PATTERNS OF JUVENILE DELINQUENCY,
   Howard B. Kaplan
3: THE IDEA OF POLICE,
   Carl Klockars
4: CRIME AND VICTIMIZATION DATA,
   Robert M. O'Brien

Additional volumes currently in development.

Crime and Victimization Data

ROBERT M. O'BRIEN

Volume 4.
Law and Criminal Justice Series

SAGE PUBLICATIONS Beverly Hills London New Delhi

For information address:

SAGE Publications, Inc.
275 South Beverly Drive
Beverly Hills, California 90212

SAGE Publications India Pvt. Ltd.
M-32 Market
Greater Kailash I
New Delhi 110 048 India

SAGE Publications Ltd
28 Banner Street
London EC1Y 8QE
England

Printed in the United States of America

Library of Congress Cataloging in Publication Data

O'Brien, Robert.
   Crime and victimization data.

   (Law and criminal justice series ; v. 4)
   Bibliography: p.
   Includes index.
   1. Criminal statistics--United States. I. Title.
II. Series.
HV6787.027   1985   364'.973'021   84-29835
ISBN 0-8039-2235-3
ISBN 0-8039-2236-1 (pbk.)

FIRST PRINTING

CONTENTS

PREFACE

Everyone in the United States is bombarded with statistical data telling us everything from the most popular candidates and toothpastes to the unemployment rate and median cost of a new house. Additionally, each year in September we are informed how the nation fared in its fight against crime. As I write this sentence, I have just heard on the radio that crime in the United States dropped by 7% during the past year. In fact, the rate dropped for all Part I crimes except rape. What am I to make of these latest statistics? Has the rate of rape leveled off while the rate of aggravated assault is dropping? Or are women reporting a higher percentage of the rapes that occur while the police are recording a larger percentage of the rapes reported to them? These sorts of questions are important not only to social scientists but also to policy-makers and "informed citizens." An upturn in the rate of rapes may call for new methods of dealing with the problem (e.g., rape crisis units with female officers), the introduction of innovative legislation, or a vote by citizens for stiffer penalties. Similarly, perceptions of "crime waves," the "dark figure" of unrecorded crime, and the "typical characteristics" of criminal offenders influence citizens, social researchers, and policy-makers.

Surprisingly, basic facts such as whether or not a crime wave has occurred or the differential rates of involvement of males (versus females), blacks (versus whites), and lower-class (versus upper-class) youth in conventional property and violent crimes are not agreed upon. Most distressing of all, the substantive results of research often depend on the particular source of the crime data used in the research. For example, population density and aggravated assault rates are positively related using *Uniform Crime Reports* data for 26 cities, but are negatively related when National Crime Survey data are used for the same 26 cities. This is only one of many "method dependent" results that exists.

This book critically examines three major sources of data on crime in the United States: the *Uniform Crime Reports* (based on crimes known to the police), the National Crime Surveys (based on the reports of victims in response to survey questions) and self-reports (based on the responses of offenders to survey questions).

First, the historical development of crime statistics in the United States is reviewed (Chapter 1). In Chapters 2-4, I discuss how crime statistics are gathered from each of these three sources, what these data include (geographical regions, demographic information about offenders and victims, and so on), and what they exclude. In these chapters the major problems with data generated by each method are examined and examples of their "reasonable" use are provided. In Chapter 5 crime data from the National Crime Surveys, *Uniform Crime Reports*, and self-report studies are compared. Here the points of agreement and disagreement for these data sources are carefully examined. Where there is disagreement, an attempt is made to explain its occurrence (e.g., why do the *Uniform Crime Reports* and National Crime Survey sources disagree with respect to the absolute crime rates while agreeing about the relative involvement of males and females in crimes). In Chapter 6 the implications of these comparisons for social scientists and policy-makers are explored and suggestions are made for both the improved use of these data and the upgrading of criminal statistics.

This work evolved out of research conducted with David Decker and David Shichor on criminal victimization in 26 large American cities. As that research progressed, I became increasingly interested in the quality of the crime data with which we were working. This book is a product of that interest. I would like to thank David Shichor as my "mentor" in criminology and both Davids for being stimulating research and writing companions and colleagues. A final note of thanks is due to Vicki Van Nortwick, who put up with numerous rough drafts of this manuscript. Somehow, she deciphered most of my scribblings.

1

INTRODUCTION

In the United States alone, tens of millions of dollars are spent on the compilation of crime statistics each year.[1] Thousands of person hours are expended in this effort and countless thousands more in examining and analyzing the resulting figures.

Why is this effort expended? The reasons are numerous and diverse, ranging from the practical, day-to-day applications of law enforcement agencies to testing criminological theories and the information needs of policy-makers both inside and outside of the criminal justice system. Within police deparments, decisions regarding the allocation of resources and staffing and the distribution of patrols are made with the help of crime reports. Police chiefs and other decision-makers must decide which areas of the city need additional security, if patrol cars should have one or two officers, the need for a special rape crisis division, whether to initiate a "crackdown" on burglary, and so on. Crime statistics for specific areas are used as one of several inputs for these decisions. At higher levels of government, crime statistics are used to argue for a greater (or lesser) allocation of funds to the criminal justice system or for changes in the judiciary or parole systems.

A step removed from these most directly applied uses of crime statistics are their uses in evaluating the effectiveness of crime control programs (e.g., a gun control program or a program that advertises that those using a gun in the commission of a crime will be sent to prison). Crime statistics may be used to evaluate the effects of a change in lighting or the increase of police patrols on the rate of burglary in a business area. They have been used to evaluate the effect of capital punishment on the rate at which murders are committed, the effectiveness of police departments, and to project future crime trends.

Crime statistics help establish the basic social facts of crime. For example, how does the crime rate vary by the age, sex, race, and income level of offenders and/or victims? How does it vary by the time of day, area of the city, or region of the country? How are the relationships between individuals (e.g., strangers, friends, relatives) related to the rates at which crimes are committed? These social facts form the building blocks for theories of criminal behavior and provide evidence by which these theories may be evaluated. There would be no need to explain the higher rate of crime commission among males if their rate were not higher than that of females or if their rate of offense appeared to be higher due only to the "chivalrous" treatment of female offenders by the police, victims, and/or witnesses. There would be no need to explain the relation between population density and the rate of aggravated assault, if it were only an artifact of the way crime rates are measured.

We should not, however, draw too rigid a distinction between the applied and less immediately applied uses of crime statistics. Social facts and theories affect policies and decisions within the criminal justice system as well as the design of crime contol programs.[2] An additional important use of crime statistics is that of informing citizens of the nature and extent of crime and, thus, influencing their support for various governmental policies. For example, if 20 out of every 1,000 women are likely to be victims of rape in a year rather than 2 in 1,000, this should affect citizen support for programs aimed at aiding the victims of rape, preventing rapes, and so on. Or, again, crime statistics may indicate that a large proportion of all homicides involve relatives and the use of handguns, and this may influence citizens' attitudes concerning gun control. In any case, citizens in a democracy should be well informed, as law and its enforcement are central areas of governmental social control.

SOURCES OF CRIME DATA

In this book the three major sources of statistics on crime in the United States are examined, evaluated, and compared. Historically, the first of these sources to be developed were the *Uniform Crime Reports* (circa 1930), the second, self-reports (during the 1940s and 1950s), and the last, sample surveys of the victims of crime (circa 1960). In the sections that follow, each of these sources of crime data is placed in historical context.[3]

Uniform Crime Reports

The Uniform Crime Reporting system was initiated by the International Association of Police Chiefs (IACP), which, during the 1920s, created a committee on uniform crime records (FBI, 1983). Their task was to create a crime reporting system that would be uniform across various police jurisdictions as, at that time, no two states defined all major crimes alike. After several drafts, based on the examination of the criminal codes of several states, a final version was published as *Uniform Crime Reporting* (IACP, 1929). In 1929 a number of police departments began collecting *Uniform Crime Reports (UCR)* crime data that was collected by the IACP and compiled by the FBI. By the middle of 1930, Congress passed a bill creating the Division of Identification and Information within the FBI with the duty of acquiring, collecting, classifying, and preserving criminal identification and other crime records. In 1930 400 cities, representing 20 million people, sent reports to the FBI (Maltz, 1977), and by 1983 the FBI received reports (that are still voluntary) from law enforcement agencies representing 226 million people, or 97% of the total population as established by the Bureau of the Census (FBI, 1983). These reports are compiled annually by the FBI and published as *Crime in the United States*. They are commonly referred to as the *Uniform Crime Reports*. In Chapter 2 these reports are examined in detail, including: how they are gathered; the crimes they cover and those they exclude; some of the problems with the data generated in these reports; and some appropriate uses for these data.

The adequacy of crime data published in the *UCR*s has been questioned by criminologists. After all, not all crimes are reported to or discovered by the police. Until offenders are arrested or identified, it is impossible to know their sex, age, or race. Any institutional bias of police departments, individual bias by police officers, or bias on the part of victims will affect the rate at which crimes are reported and recorded and, thus, the relative numbers of male to female, white to nonwhite, young to old, or rich to poor offenders. For these and other reasons that are reviewed in the next chapter, the accuracy of *UCR* data has been challenged. In addition, the *UCR*s fail to provide detailed information about offenders that would be valuable to researchers and policymakers: for example, the number of other offenses committed by the offender, the offender's academic record, attitudes toward their offense, relationships with parents, interest in school, consumption of alcohol, and so on. Obtaining this sort of information is possible using research based on the self-reports of offenders.

Self-Report Studies

Self-report (SR) studies involve asking individuals whether they have committed one or more of a list of delinquent/criminal acts. Although there were a few exploratory attempts designed to measure delinquent behavior using self-reports during the 1940s (Porterfield, 1946; Wallerstein and Wyle, 1947), the first full-scale study was conducted in the 1950s by Short and Nye (1957). These studies quickly grew in popularity and became the preferred research strategy of those interested in the causes of individual delinquency. SR studies differed from *UCR* data in the types of "criminal behavior" on which they focused. Whereas the *UCR*s focused on relatively serious law violating behavior, SR studies focused on delinquent behaviors such as skipping school without a legitimate excuse, defying parental authority, or driving a car without a driver's license or permit. As we shall see in Chapter 4, the results of these early SR studies often seem to contradict *UCR* data. This is true, for example, for the proportion of crimes committed by males (versus females) and blacks (versus whites) as well as for the absolute rate of criminal behavior.

More recent studies have used refined SR techniques and asked about more serious types of offenses. In these studies, some of the differences between *UCR* and SR crime rates for the proportion of males to females, black to white, and so on, are greatly diminished (Elliott and Ageton, 1980; Hindelang et al., 1981). Furthermore, although most SR studies have involved samples of relatively small populations, there have been two SR studies conducted on national samples (Elliott et al., 1983; Gold and Reimer, 1975). In Chapter 4 the SR method of gathering data will be examined and its problems and potentials discussed.

National Crime Surveys (NCS)

A third major approach to the study of crime involves surveys of victims. Rather than relying on records of police departments (*UCR*) or on the admissions of criminal behavior of offenders (SR), victimization studies rely on the recall of the victims of crime. These surveys ask samples of individuals, household heads, or respondents representing businesses whether they have been the victims of criminal acts during a specified period of time.

The first surveys of victims in the United States were conducted in the mid-1960s. These initial surveys were sponsored by the President's Commission on Law Enforcement and Administration of Justice. Among the largest of these were those conducted in Washington, D.C. by the Bureau of Social Science Research (Biderman et al., 1967), in Boston, Chicago, and Washington, D.C. by the Institute for Social Research at the University of Michigan (Reiss, 1967), and for a nationwide sample of 10,000 households by the National Opinion Research Center at the University of Chicago (Ennis, 1967). One of the most dramatic findings of these victimization studies was that the crime rates reported in the *UCR*s were only one-half to one-third of those based on the reports of victims. In the early 1970s a number of surveys were conducted to answer methodological questions that had been raised by these and other victimization surveys. For instance, how likely were respondents to report the crimes they suffered to survey interviewers? When asking respondents about criminal victimizations, should interviewers inquire about crimes occurring during the past three months, six months, or year? How should questions be worded in order to obtain the most valid answers? To answer these questions, a number of pilot studies were designed by the Law Enforcement Assistance Administration (LEAA) in cooperation with the U.S. Bureau of the Census.

These surveys were conducted in Baltimore (U.S. Bureau of the Census, 1970a); Washington, D.C. (U.S. Bureau of the Census, 1970b); San Jose, California (LEAA, 1972, 1974); Cleveland and Akron, Ohio (Dodge and Turner, 1971); and nationally as part of the Census Bureau's Quarterly Household Surveys (Dodge and Turner, 1971). They represent an extensive effort at validating and improving the techniques used in victimization surveys.

After the completion of the LEAA/Census pilot surveys, the National Crime Surveys (NCSs) were initiated. These surveys were composed of two different sets: the city samples and the national sample. In the city samples 26 large central cities were surveyed (13 of these were surveyed twice). In each city a stratified sample of about 10,000 households was surveyed and a probability sample of from 1,000 to 5,000 businesses (depending on the size of the city). The city surveys were discontinued after 1975. The national survey was initiated in 1972 with samples of approximately 60,000 households (containing some 136,000 individuals) and about 15,000 businesses. The national surveys of households (but not businesses) are still being conducted (both surveys are examined in detail in Chapter 3).

MULTIPLE MEASURES OF CRIME

The importance of multiple measures is widely recognized in the social sciences. The general idea is that each method of measurement (e.g., *UCR*, NCS, or SR crime rates) has its own biases and inaccuracies. If the results of these methods can be compared, however, it may be possible to evaluate the effects of the biases in each of them, to evaluate their accuracy, and possibly to make adjustments for some of their deficiencies.

In the case of crime rate estimates based on *UCR*, NCS and SR data, the ideal situation would be to find an absolute convergence between rates based on each of these methods; that is, to find that crime rates for cities as estimated by each of these methods is the same or nearly the same. If this did not occur, we might hope for the relative convergence of different crime rate measures. For example, the *UCR* and NCS estimates of crime rates might at least rank cities in the same order or agree concerning the percentage of crimes committed by males in the United States. If crime data collected by different methods agree, it increases our confidence in the data. The particular type of convergence (absolute or relative) is important in suggesting areas in which the data might validly be used. For example, if city crime rates show relative convergence for *UCR* and NCS data, this would encourage the use of these data in analyses comparing the relative rates of crime across cities. Furthermore, this relative convergence would support the appropriateness of correlational studies (e.g., the correlation of population density and crime rates) using cities as the units of analysis. This particular form of convergence, however, would not indicate that the absolute extent of crime within cities was accurately measured.

Put another way, if different ways of measuring crime produce the same results, our confidence in the results is increased. The type of convergence, however, is important in determining the type of uses of the data that are supported. Chapter 5 will compare the results produced by *UCR*, NCS, and SR methods in terms of the absolute rates of crime, the demographic characteristics of offenders, the ecological distribution of crime, and over-time trends in crime rates.

The final chapter summarizes the implications of the examination of *UCR*, NCS, and SR crime rate data. For example, what are the implications for policy-makers, researchers, and citizens? To what extent are the results of research dependent on the methods used to collect crime data? How can the methods used to collect data be improved? In the next chapter, I will focus on the oldest of the three methods of gathering crime data, the *Uniform Crime Reports*.

SUMMARY

Several important uses of data on crime and criminal victimization have been discussed and the three major sources of these data have been introduced. Historically, the first to be developed were the *UCR*s, followed by the SRs, and then by the NCSs. Each collects data on crime from a different source; *UCR*s are based on crimes known to the police, SRs are based on the admission of offending behavior by respondents, and NCSs are based on the reports of respondents who say they have been victimized.

The multiple measures of crime that result from these three sources make it possible to assess tentatively the validity of data from each of them and to ascertain whether the results of analyses based on these different data sources produce similar findings or whether the results are "method dependent." This chapter sets the structure for those that follow. In Chapters 2-4 each of the three major data sources is examined in terms of the information it includes and excludes, problems with the data, and some reasonable uses for the data. Chapter 5 compares the results produced by *UCR*, NCS, and SR methods, and Chapter 6 summarizes the implications of the analysis for the uses of these data.

NOTES

1. The Office of Justice Assistance Research and Statistics, the successor agency to the Law Enforcement and Assistance Administration, spent $14 million on statistical programs in 1980, and lists another $21 million under the heading of research and statistics (Flanagan and McLeod, 1983: Table 1.10). In 1977 Garofalo estimated that the field costs alone of a victim survey conducted by a local agency was $16 to $35 per interview. The NCS involves interviews with members of over 60,000 households annually. In the same year Garofalo reported that the *New York Times* estimated that $53 million had been spent on victim surveys to that date.

2. The President's Commission on Law Enforcement and the Administration of Justice was created, in part, to use research as the basis for informing policy decisions and for designing further research that would test the effectiveness of crime control programs.

3. There are several excellent historical reviews of the *UCRs* and NCSs (see, especially, Maltz, 1977; U.S. Department of Justice, 1981b). Hindelang (1976) provides a detailed review of victimization surveys and the first section of *Crime in the United States* (FBI, 1983) provides a short historical review of the Uniform Crime Reporting Program. A brief review of SR studies can be found in Hindelang et al. (1981).

2

UNIFORM CRIME REPORTS:
Official Data

The most widely publicized criminal statistics in the United States are those based on the *Uniform Crime Reports* (*UCR*s). When we read in the newspaper that the homicide rate in California is higher than the national average or that Detroit has the highest rate of homicide for any city over one million population in the United States, these figures are almost certainly based on *UCR* data. Immediately after these statistics are published each year in *Crime in the United States*, a rash of articles on crime trends and the relative standings of states and individual cities in terms of crime rates appear in newspapers and magazines.

THE COLLECTION OF *UCR* DATA

The Uniform Crime Reporting program was initiated in the 1930s in order to obtain more reliable crime statistics. A major obstacle to obtaining such data is that crimes are defined differently from state to state and sometimes even between jurisdictions within the same state. For example, some states have broad burglary statutes that include criminal acts that do not involve breaking and entering, whereas others require these elements. One police jurisdiction may not consider a car reported missing as stolen until it has been missing for several days, whereas another may consider it to be stolen as soon as it is reported missing. In order to make criminal statistics more comparable, the Uniform Crime Reporting Program was developed to provide uniform definitions of crimes. Law enforcement agencies in this program report crimes on the basis of these definitions. Currently, the *Uniform Crime Reporting Handbook* (FBI, 1980) details procedures for classifying and scoring offenses. The purpose of these procedures is to make data on crimes as comparable as possible, from year to year (month to month) within jurisdictions and from one jurisdiction to another.

The data collected under the Uniform Crime Reporting Program are tabulated by local law enforcement agencies (police departments, sheriff's departments, etc.) using rules specified in the crime reporting handbook. These tabulations are then sent either directly to the FBI or to a state-level UCR program. In 1983 there were 41 state-level programs. These programs, as well as the FBI, are responsible for providing some degree of quality control for the data. These quality checks include examining each report for arithmetical accuracy, for patterns of rates that differ from similar reporting agencies, and for trends that are unusual.

Participation in the UCR program is voluntary except that some states with state-level programs have mandatory reporting requirements. In 1983 law enforcement agencies representing 226 million people participated in the program. These agencies represented over 98% of the United States population living in SMSAs, 94% of the population in "other cities," and over 90% of the rural population. Overall, this represents 97% of the total population of the United States (FBI, 1983).

WHAT *UCR* DATA INCLUDE

The *UCR*s provide a wealth of data with wide geographical coverage. The crimes reported in the *UCR*s are broken down into two types of crimes. Seven crimes originally were selected for inclusion in the *UCR Crime Index* because: (1) they are most likely to be reported to police; (2) police investigations easily can establish whether a crime has occurred; (3) they occur in all geographical areas; (4) they occur with sufficient frequency to provide an adequate basis of comparison; and (5) they are serious by nature and/or volume (U.S. Department of Justice, 1981b).

The Part I crimes that make up the crime index are murder and nonnegligent manslaughter, forcible rape, robbery, aggravated assault, burglary, larceny-theft, and motor vehicle theft. In 1979 arson was added to the crime index by congressional mandate. The definitions of these crimes as they appear in the annual publication of *UCR* statistics, *Crime in the United States*, are given in Appendix 1 (Part A). Detailed rules for coding crime incidents into these categories are used by reporting agencies and are found in the *Uniform Crime Reporting Handbook* (FBI, 1980).

To determine the number of *UCR* index crimes that have occurred, law enforcement agencies must follow a special "counting rule." They count only the most serious crime that occurred during a single incident. For this purpose, the seriousness of a crime corresponds to the order of the index offenses in Appendix 1 (Part A). For example, if a woman enters a house, steals a camera, and, when she encounters the owner, threatens him or her with a gun and steals his or her car, she has committed a number of index crimes; but the *UCR* would record only the most serious—robbery. Arson is an exception to this reporting rule, and is reported even if other index crimes have occurred.

The crime index is a simple sum of seven Part I offenses (arson is excluded). In addition, two other indices routinely are reported by the FBI in *Crime in the United States*. The first is a violent crime index composed of murder and nonnegligent manslaughter, forcible rape, robbery, and aggravated assault. The second is a property crime index made up of burglary, larceny-theft, and motor vehicle theft. As with the crime index, these indices are simple sums of the crimes included in them.

These crime indices can be misleading, as they weight crimes equally no matter what their type. For instance, each larceny-theft is weighted the same as a murder. Thus, if there was an increase of 40 incidents in the murder/nonnegligent manslaughter category, these incidents would be overwhelmed by a decrease in the number of larceny thefts of 400. As a rule of thumb, it is best to examine the Part I crimes separately, rather than in index form. Otherwise, a decrease in serious crimes (Part I crimes), as suggested by a reduction in the crime index, may mean only a decrease in larceny-thefts, which are the most common index crimes, whereas murder and rape may have increased substantially.

Table 2.1 is a modified example of *UCR* data as it appears in *Crime in the United States* (FBI, 1982). The first column, labeled offense, designates the index, the two subindices of violent and property crimes, and each of the crimes that make up the crime index (Part I crimes). The next column lists the estimated number of crimes and the third reports crime rate per 100,000 inhabitants. The final four columns present (respectively) the percentage change in the number of crimes and the crime rate over the previous year, and over the last decade.

The number of Part I crimes in Table 2.1 is based on "crimes known to the police." These include any crimes that come to the attention of law enforcement agencies. Most of these are reported by victims, but also are based on crimes reported by witnesses, discovered by the police, and so on. Before potential criminal incidents are recorded as officially known to the police, they must go through a police unfounding

TABLE 2.1
Number, Rate, and Percentage Change in Crimes

Offense	Estimated Crime 1983		Percentage Change Over 1982		Percentage Change Over 1974	
	Number	Rate per 100,000 Inhabitants	Number	Rate per 100,000 Inhabitants	Number	Rate per 100,000 Inhabitants
Crime index total	12,070,200	5,158.6	−6.7	−7.7	+17.7	+6.4
Violent crime	1,237,980	529.1	−4.9	−5.9	+27.0	+14.7
Property crime	10,832,200	4,629.5	−6.9	−7.9	+16.7	+5.5
Murder	19,310	8.3	−8.1	−8.8	−6.8	−15.3
Forcible rape	78,920	33.7	—	−1.2	+42.5	+28.6
Robbery	500,220	213.8	−8.4	−9.4	+13.1	+2.2
Aggravated assault	639,530	273.3	−2.4	−3.4	+40.2	+26.6
Burglary	3,120,800	1,333.8	−9.2	−10.2	+2.7	−7.2
Larceny-theft	6,707,000	2,866.5	−6.0	−7.0	+27.4	+15.1
Motor vehicle theft	1,004,400	429.3	−5.1	−6.1	+2.8	−7.1

SOURCE: Adapted from *Crime in the United States* (FBI, 1983: 41)

procedure to determine whether the police think a "crime" has occurred. If they are unfounded or determined not to be Part I crimes, they are eliminated from the count.

When the UCR system was first established, there was debate over the value of collecting data on crimes known to the police. Some argued that these data would not be useful because they would not include information about the sex, race, age, and other characteristics of offenders. These characteristics could only be known once the offender was arrested. Furthermore, it was argued that the determination of whether a crime had actually been committed was better made after an arrest (and, some might argue, after a conviction) had occurred. The prevailing side, however, argued that "the value of a crime for index purposes decreases as the distance from the crime itself in terms of procedure increases" (Sellin, 1931: 346). This principle, sometimes known as Sellin's dictum, was based on the idea that the screening process involved in the criminal justice system would hide from view a large number of crimes for which no arrest was made or for which no conviction was obtained. Thus, in general, for crimes known to the police there is no data on demographic or other characteristics of offenders.

The case of murder, however, is an exception to this general rule. For this crime the *UCR*s provide some detailed data. For example, they present information on the age, sex, race, and ethnic origin of the murder victim as well as the race, sex, and ethnic origin of the offender when known. The race and ethnic origin of victims and offenders is cross classified. The types of weapon (e.g., firearm, knife, poison, explosives, fire, or fists) used in the offense are tabulated. The relationship between the offender and victim (e.g., wife, husband, son, daughter, boyfriend, girlfriend, neighbor, or stranger) is described when known (in 28.2% of the cases in 1983 the relationship was not known). Such details on victims and offenders are valuable, but are largely absent in the *UCR*s for other types of crime.

Some details, besides estimated number and rates, are provided for other crimes. The type of weapon used (firearms, knife, other) is presented for robberies and aggravated assaults. The location of robberies is broken down into street, gas station, residence, commercial house, convenience store, bank, and other. Burglaries are classified as residential or nonresidential. Larceny is broken down into several categories (e.g., purse snatching, pocket picking, shoplifting, and theft of bicycles). The object of arson is described as motor vehicle, single occupancy residential, other residential, storage, and so on. These sorts of breakdowns, however, are provided only for the total United States population and not for smaller geographic areas.

The Part I offenses known to the police are reported each month as well as the number of index crimes that have been "cleared." Crimes either are cleared when an arrest is made and at least one person is charged with the crime (clearance by arrest) or are cleared by exceptional means when police know the identity and location of the suspect and have information to support arrest, charging, and prosecution, but are prevented from taking action by circumstances outside of their control (e.g., the suspect is dead or is in custody in another jurisdiction, or the victim refuses to cooperate; see U.S. Department of Justice, 1981a). The *UCR* publications report the clearance rate for index offenses. This rate is the number of crimes cleared divided by the number of offenses known to the police, expressed as a percentage.

The *UCR*s include data on offenders arrested for Part I offenses. These data include the age, sex, race, and ethnic origin of the persons arrested. Although these data are at a farther distance from the crime itself than crimes known to the police (in terms of criminal justice procedures), they do supply information on offender characteristics. For Part II offenses only arrest data are available. These offenses are listed in Appendix 1 (Part B) in order of their assumed seriousness. Again, in multiple offense situations the published arrest data indicate only the most serious charge resulting from a criminal incident at the time of the arrest.

The major source for the *UCR* data that are sent to the FBI is the individual law enforcement agency and this provides the lowest level of aggregation for crime statistics (number and rates of crimes) for these data. In the yearly publication of these statistics, *Crime in the United States*, these data are presented for cities, counties, states (plus the District of Columbia), and regions (northeastern, north, central, southern, and western). *UCR* data are also reported using three community-type aggregations. The first of these, Standard Metropolitan Statistics Areas (SMSAs), made up about 76% of the total population of the United States in 1983. In addition to core cities of over 50,000 inhabitants, the SMSAs include surrounding suburban cities (of less than 50,000) and suburban counties. The second community-type is "other cities," most of which are not incorporated. These comprised 10% of the United States population in 1983. The last type of community consists of rural counties, which are defined as those counties outside of SMSAs. In 1983 they comprised 14% of the national population. Their population excludes areas covered by city police agencies. *Crime in the United States* also breaks down the number of crimes and crime rates by population groups based on size. For example, Group I (cities of over 250,000 inhabitants), Group II (cities of 100,000 to 249,999 inhabitants), Group IX (suburban counties).

The geographic coverage provided by the *UCR* and published in *Crime in the United States* is quite wide. There is no other source of data on crime in the United States that provides such detailed geographic coverage. There is no other source of data from which to estimate the yearly crime rates for Eugene, Oregon or Madison, Wisconsin. These and most other cities have not been surveyed in order to estimate rates of victimization and to do so would take samples of thousands of households. Thus, when information on crime rates in most localities or in the 200 largest U.S. cities is needed, we turn of necessity to the *UCR*s. These reports, however, do not provide data on many variables of interest to administrators, politicians, policy-makers, citizens, and researchers.

WHAT *UCR* DATA EXCLUDE

By the very nature of the data collection approach employed in the *UCR*s, certain data of interest are not collected. For example, data based on known offenses generally does not include the sex, age, race, and ethnic group of the offender (or other relevant characteristics such as the offender's educational and family background). This information is not available until the stage of arrest (although with some effort the sex, race, and even age of offenders could be estimated for crimes in which victims and offenders come into contact). In fact, limited data are available on offender characteristics in the case of murder.

Data are not collected on the victims of crime (again with the exception of murder). Thus, we cannot estimate the number of assault victims who are women or blacks. It would be possible to obtain information on the characteristics of victims, but such information is not gathered by the *UCR*s. A cross-classification of offender and victim characteristics would add to our understanding of crime. These data would be of use to policy-makers, researchers, and others interested in crime and crime rates.

The data reported by the *UCR*s are aggregate-level data. Even at the lowest level of aggregation (the law enforcement agency), there is no way to trace a single individual through the criminal justice system. We cannot find out, for example, what happens to a 22-year-old hispanic female who murders her daughter. We cannot follow her case from offense to arrest, through her court case, sentencing, and possible incarceration. Such a data base exists in California's Offender Based Transaction System, but is not part of the UCR program.

Even when data are available in the reports that are sent to the FBI, often it is difficult or impossible to obtain data at the level of aggregation desired. For example, although arrest data are reported at the city, county, SMSA, and state level, data on the sex, age, race, and ethnic origin of offenders are not reported on these levels. Furthermore, it would be convenient to have published tables that cross-classify arrests by sex, age, race, or ethnic origin; however, only tables cross-classifying Part I arrests by sex and age for the total U.S. population are available. Adding these tables to a publication such as *Crime in the United States* would be impractical because they would occupy hundreds of additional pages, but these data should be made available and easily accessible for policy-makers and researchers (perhaps in a special publication supplied to federal depository libraries and available through interlibrary loan).

These more detailed breakdowns sometimes may be obtained for states that publish their own crime reports. For example, California published *Crime and Delinquency in California* (Deukmejian, 1981), in which arrest statistics for various crimes are cross-classified by the age, sex, and race/ethnic group of the offender. Even here, these types of breakdowns for smaller geographic regions are not reported.

Although the list of crimes included in the *UCR*s is long (see Appendix 1, Parts A and B) there are some notable omissions. The reports do not include federal crimes such as kidnapping or depriving individuals of their civil rights. They also do not include many types of white-collar crimes that seldom come to the attention of police.

PROBLEMS WITH *UCR* DATA

A key to understanding and evaluating data on crime rates, no matter by what method they are gathered, is to analyze how these data are produced. Here, some major elements involved in the production of official criminal statistics are examined. These elements are discussed under the headings of factors affecting the reporting of crimes and factors affecting the recording of crimes; however, it should be noted that these elements are not entirely independent of one another.

Factors Affecting the Reporting of Crimes

Both Part I and Part II crimes usually require what has been labeled a "reactive mobilization process" (Black, 1973), before they come to the attention of the police. That is, they usually come to the attention of the police through "reaction" to citizens' complaints. Thus, for these crimes, the reporting behavior of citizens plays a major role in determining the number of crimes known to the police.

Whether or not citizens report a crime to the police depends (in part) on several features of the criminal act itself. Probably the most important element is the seriousness of the crime. For example, an old bicycle stolen from a garage or a shoving match at a bar may not seem important enough to report. The theft of an expensive stereo set that had been stored in the same garage or the stabbing of a person in a barroom fight, however, are much more likely to be reported by the victim, witness, or investigating officer. Some of the best evidence available concerning the correlation between crime seriousness and reporting comes from the National Crime Surveys (NCSs). In these surveys respondents are asked a series of questions to ascertain whether they have been the victim of serious crimes. If they say they have been, they are asked whether they reported their victimization to the police. It is then possible to estimate the percentage of victimizations that were reported to the police. In 1980 75% of robberies and attempted robberies with injuries that involved serious assault were reported to the police, whereas only 64% of those involving minor assaults were reported. Only 60% of robberies without injuries and 35% of attempted robberies without injuries were reported. In the case of assault, 60% of aggravated assaults with injury and 40% of simple assaults were reported. For buglaries that involved forcible entry, 73% were reported, whereas those that involved unlawful entry without force were reported only 43% of the time. Finally, larcenies of $50 or more were reported 45% of the time, and those under $50 were reported only 14% of the time (Flanagan and McLeod, 1983: Table 3.1: 292).

The decision to report or not to report a crime also depends on the type of crime. For example, rape and attempted rape are reported 43% of the time. This is, indeed, a serious crime, but other factors (embarrassment, relationship to the offender, expectations of negative police reactions, and so on) depress the reporting rate for this crime. On the other hand, motor vehicle theft is reported 69% of the time (86% for completed motor vehicle thefts and 33% for attempted thefts). In the case of vehicle thefts, the motivation for reporting the crime may include factors other than its inherent seriousness (e.g., to collect insurance).

The NCS asks respondents who did not report crimes to the police why they failed to do so. Table 2.2 shows the reported reasons for some selected crimes. A major reason given for not reporting crimes is a perception that nothing could be done, the victimization is not important enough, or the police would not want to be bothered. This perception may occur when the offender is a stranger or, in cases of stolen property, when the chances of recovery are probably slight and the items either are not of great value or are not covered by insurance. Many of the incidents seem to be viewed as private matters for which respondents choose not to invoke the law. This was true for 22% of the rapes. Also, 14% of the rape victims did not report the incident for fear of reprisal.

The relationship between the victim and offender is another factor that has been widely cited as influencing the victim's decision to report a criminal victimization. Using data from the National Opinion Research Center's victimization study conducted in 1966, Block (1974) presents some evidence bearing on this question. He found for assault victimizations that when the offender was a stranger, 66% of the victims reported the crime to the police; when the offender was known to the victim, 51% reported the incident; and when the victim was a relative, only 44% reported the incident. These findings, in part, explain the

TABLE 2.2
Percentage of Victimizations Not Reported to the Police
by Type of Victimization and Reason Given for Not Reporting,
1980 NCS Survey

	Rape and Attempted Rape	Personal Robbery	Household Burglary	Motor Vehicle Theft
Nothing could be done	18	16	22	22
Victimization not important enough	7	13	26	15
Police would not want to be bothered	9	12	9	7
Did not want to take the time	0	6	2	3
It was a private matter	22	16	8	14
Fear of reprisal	14	6	1	0
Victimization was reported to someone else	14	6	6	3
Other	38	42	43	51
Not ascertained	2	5	3	4

NOTE: Data are from Flanagan and McLeod (1983: 302, Table 3.6).

relatively low percentage of rapes (43%) as well as assaults (45%) reported to the police.

Many additional factors have been cited as reasons victims may not report crimes to the police. Victims may not realize that a crime has been committed. For instance, an item may be stolen but presumed lost. There may be no victim in the usual sense with crimes that are "victimless." The victim may fear self-incrimination. The victim may fear the personal consequences of the criminal justice proceedings: cross examination, public condemnation, or publicity (Decker et al., 1982).[1] Most criminologists agree that the factors outlined above result in an underreporting of crime incidents to law enforcement agencies.

Factors Affecting the Recording of Crimes

The recording of an act in police records as a "crime known to the police" and the follow-up of arrest are dependent on a number of factors: for example, organizational pressures to get the crime rate up or down, police officer and offender interactions, and the professionalism of particular police departments.

Law enforcement agencies exist in a sociopolitical environment that often evaluates their performances and needs on the basis of crime statistics that the law enforcement agencies generate themselves. Their detection of crimes may be interpreted as a sign of their effectiveness in dealing with the crime problem. Furthermore, their requests for funding and expansion often are based on perceptions of the extent of the crime problem. For example, crime waves may suggest the need for increased funding of police departments, which can result in organizational pressures to report crimes (Chambliss, 1984; Selke and Pepinsky, 1982). Under political pressures, law enforcement agencies may "crack down" on certain crimes, such as gambling, prostitution, or drugs (Defleur, 1975). The result may be an increase in the detection or recording of these crimes, which is not based on an increase in offending behavior (Bell, 1960; DeFleur, 1975; Sheley and Hanlon, 1978; Wheeler, 1967). For instance, Sheley and Hanlon describe how a crackdown on heroin traffic in a city of about 200,000 led to a slight increase in the number of arrests during the crackdown period and then a substantial drop in the number of arrests when the campaign was terminated. They speculate that the drop in arrests was due to the fact that the heroin traffic was moved deeper underground. An unintended consequence of the heroin crackdown was an increase in the number of arrests for marijuana.

DeFleur (1975), in a historical study of drug arrests in Chicago, concluded that the distributions of arrest statistics for both white and nonwhite offenders over both time and geographic location reflect systematic biases in the operation of police assigned to the narcotics division. These biases are so severe that researchers ought not rely on these data as indices of drug behavior. Many of the shifts in drug activity over time can be explained by increases in the number of officers assigned to narcotics law enforcement. During the 1940s most of the narcotics law enforcement was carried out by 5 or 6 officers. In 1951 a separate narcotics unit was created and within two or three years it included 59 officers, with 30 to 40 more in local districts. Another important change in enforcement occurred after the 1968 riots in Chicago. Officers were ordered to avoid work in the areas in which blacks lived. This affected the relative rates of arrests for whites and nonwhites and the geographic distribution of drug arrests in Chicago.

A number of researchers (e.g., Seidman and Couzens, 1974; Selke and Pepinsky, 1982) also have noted that law enforcement agencies may respond at times to pressures to get the crime rate down. For instance, Seidman and Couzens (1974) noted an abrupt drop in the percentage of larcenies of $50 or more in response to the installation of a new police chief who threatened to replace police commanders who were unable to reduce crime in their jurisdictions. The importance of the more (or less) than $50 criterion was that larcenies of less than $50 were not reported in the FBI crime index. Thus, by the simple expedient of estimating the value of stolen goods to be slightly less than $50, it was possible for law enforcement personnel to get the official (*UCR*) crime rate down.

A recent study of three police departments using time-series data shows the effects of organizational changes within the departments on the crime rates produced (McCleary et al., 1982). In one department an abrupt drop in the number of *UCR* burglaries appeared at the onset of a 21-month period in which all burglary complaints were formally investigated by detectives. The previous procedure had involved the filing of simple field reports by uniformed officers. When the experimental program involving formal investigation ended 21 months later, the *UCR* burglary rate went up again. The explanation lies in the better classification of events as burglaries by detectives with time to investigate. In a second police department they found a dramatic increase in the crime rate that occurred when an incumbent police chief retired. In a third city the crime rate increased when specific work shifts in the dispatch bureau, which had been supervised by sergeants, had the sergeants removed. The result was an increase in the number of "service calls" for which police were dispatched and a corresponding increase in reported crime.

Differences in state laws and local enforcement policies and practices are important determinants of recorded crime rates. As Beattie (1960) points out, there are really 51 different sets of laws defining crimes (50 states plus the District of Columbia). A recent publication of the U.S. Department of Justice (1981a) compares two states in terms of differences in behavior that are labeled as burglary. In one state breaking and entering were required, whereas in the second state only entering was required. In the first state only occupied and unoccupied dwelling houses or sleeping apartments could be counted as burglarized, whereas in the second state houses, rooms, shops, barns, stables, tents, and outhouses were included. In the first state the act must be committed during the night. Obviously, at the state level the crime of "burglary" includes different acts depending on the state in which it occurs. In the example above, the first state has an offense labeled "breaking and entering" that covers commercial buildings and would be included in *UCR* burglary reports. More problematic is whether the crimes committed in outhouses, stables, and the like, that are classified as larcenies in one state and burglaries in another, would be coded in similar categories for the *UCR*. Beattie (1960) pointed to another example from California and Virginia. In California taking valuables from a locked car was defined as burglary, whereas in Virginia it was defined as larceny.

In addition to differences in state laws and certain differences in city and county ordinances, individual law enforcement agencies differ in their degree of professionalism, style of enforcement, number of police per citizen, and so on. A number of researchers have argued that the degree of professionalism may affect the number of crimes that are recorded (Beattie, 1960; Skogan, 1976; Wilson, 1978).

The problem, from the standpoint of comparability, is that more professional departments are likely to record crimes more often as they "are more interested in data collection and record keeping, for they use such information to allocate resources and evaluate personnel" (Skogan, 1976: 111). Furthermore, there should be a greater reliance on the formal rather than informal disposition of complaints in such departments. Beattie (1960) argued that the high rate of crime in Los Angeles under Chief of Police Parker was due to the high level of efficiency and dedication of the police force and not a high rate of offenses among the population. A similar conclusion was drawn by Wilson (1967) in a study of two police departments, one in the eastern United States that was relatively nonprofessional and one in the West that was highly professional (e.g., it had universalistic standards, achievement-based recruitment, and higher educational standards). He argued that in the West Coast city youths are more likely to be picked up for minor offenses and for these to be treated as major offenses that result in arrest.

In a later study involving eight cities, Wilson (1978) argued that there are at least three styles or strategies defining the role of patrol officers. The watchman style emphasizes the order maintenance function rather than the law enforcement function for crimes that are not "serious." This allows patrol officers to ignore many common minor violations that are not a threat to public order. The legalistic style may induce patrol officers to handle commonplace situations as if they were matters of law enforcement rather than order maintenance.

> A legalistic department will issue traffic tickets at a high rate, detain and arrest a high proportion of juvenile offenders, act vigorously against illicit enterprises, and make a large number of misdemeanor arrests even when, as with petty larceny, the public order has not been breached [Wilson, 1978: 172].

The service style demands that police take seriously all requests for either law enforcement or order maintenance; however, they are less likely to make an arrest than police with a legalistic style. Police intervene frequently but not formally to maintain order. Wilson suggests that the style of policing is based on factors such as the community composition: for example, the service style is likely to be found "in homogeneous, middle-class communities in which there is a high level of apparent agreement among citizens on the need for and definition of public order but in which there is no administrative demand for a legalistic style" (Wilson, 1978: 200). Or on past scandals in the department, a "reform chief must get hold of his department. To break through the governing pattern of personal relations, loyalties, and feuds to which he, as an outsider, is alien he seeks to centralize control, formalize authority and require written accounts of everything that transpires" (Wilson, 1978: 183). Whatever the reasons for different styles of policing, they make a difference in the proportion of minor offenses that are recorded. The degree to which style affects the recording of serious offenses is more problematic, but there is probably some impact on Part I offenses such as assaults.

Skogan (1976) uses a quantitative analysis to show that more professional departments (e.g., those with a larger proportion of minority officers and civilian employees, those with more employees per 10,000 residents, and those with greater dollar expenditure per capita) record a higher percentage of crimes that citizens claim to have reported to the police. He estimated the number of crimes reported to the police on the basis of crime surveys and the number of recorded crimes on the basis of *UCR*s. The correlation is positive between each of the measures of professionalism and the ratio of recorded to reported crimes for the 26 cities for which data were available. Skogan notes that this results in relatively high official rates of crime for those departments that are most highly professionalized. In fact, it results in lower clearance ratios and, thus, makes these organizations appear less effective.

Wilson (1978) argues that within police departments discretion increases as one moves down the hierarchy. This is different than the situation found in many other organizations in which the lowest level jobs are the most routine. In police work the situations encountered by the patrol officer are seldom the same and are seldom under close supervision by superiors. Furthermore, there is no clear criterion of success or productivity (unless there is pressure to get the crime rate up or down). Thus, there is a large degree of discretion with regard to the official recording of an incident as a crime.

Perhaps the best known study of the factors leading patrol officers to write official reports is that conducted by Reiss and Black. In this research a team of observers rode with police patrols in Boston, Chicago, and Washington, D.C. One report (Black, 1970) examined incidents in which the complainant was present but the suspect was not. The research question centered on the factors that lead to citizens complaints being written up as official crime reports by patrol officers (this occurred for 64% of the complaints). He found that seriousness of the alleged offenses is positively related to the filing of an official crime report as is the complainant's manifest preference for police action. The greater the relational distance between the complainant and the suspect, the greater the probability of an official report. That is, police are more likely to file official reports when the victim and offender are strangers than when they are friends or neighbors. The more deferrential the complainant, the more likely an official report. Finally, Black found no evidence of racial discrimination in crime reporting and found only some evidence that white-collar complainants for legally serious crimes are more likely to have their complaints officially recognized.

In another article, Black and Reiss (1970) report findings based on 281 police encounters with juvenile suspects (under 18 years of age). They report that almost 85% of these encounters were not officially reported as crimes. That is, "the probability is less than one-in-seven that a policeman confronting a juvenile suspect will exercise his discretion to produce an official case of juvenile delinquency" (1970: 68). They note the importance of the legal seriousness of the alleged offense and the manifest preference of the complainant, not only for recording the crime, but for deciding to arrest the suspect. Furthermore, they find that the probabilities of arrest are higher for disrespectful juveniles than those showing a moderate degree of respect; and are higher in situations in which there is either a police witness or a citizen who can provide testimony. There is evidence that black juveniles have a comparatively high arrest rate, but Black maintains that evidence showing police discrimination is lacking as this higher rate is explained by the greater rate at which blacks show disrespect for the police.[2]

Studies of police behavior have been characterized as "a series of bivariate assertions about the impact certain variables have on police behavior" (Sherman, 1980: 70). Two recent reports by Smith and Visher (1981) and Visher (1983) have examined the multivariate relationship of factors involved in police decisions to arrest suspects. They used data gathered by trained observers riding with patrol officers. These data represent 24 police departments in St. Louis, Missouri; Rochester, New York; and Tampa-St. Petersburg, Florida. They found that after controlling for a series of factors thought to have an influence on police decisions to arrest suspects, the presence of a bystander, the preference of the complainant for formal or informal action, the race of the suspect, the demeanor of the suspect (antagonistic or not), whether the suspect was a stranger or not, and whether the offense was a felony all were significantly related to police officers' decisions to arrest the suspect. Controlling for these factors, they found that neither the offender's age nor sex were important in predicting whether the offender would be arrested.

In a later article, Visher (1983) focused on the issue of gender and police arrest decisions using a variant of what has been labeled the chivalry hypothesis. Specifically, she investigated the effects of women behaving in a gender-stereotypic manner on police arrest decisions. She found some evidence that she interprets as indicating that "those female suspects who violate typical middle-class standards of traditional female characteristics and behaviors (i.e., white, older, and submissive) are not afforded any chivalrous treatment during the arrest decisions." In fact, the effects of race and age on arrest decisions are statistically significantly different for males and females with black women and young women being at greater risk. These findings indicate the importance of going beyond bivariate assertions. Furthermore, the Smith and Visher (1981) study indicates that blacks are arrested more often even when controlling for the seriousness of the offense and several other relevant variables. This is different than the conclusion drawn by Black (1970).[3]

Another study dealing with the reporting behavior of police officers was conducted by Pepinsky (1976). He found that, to a remarkable extent, police decisions to record an offense were determined by whether the dispatcher named an offense when the officer was dispatched. The operative rule seemed to be that "no offense is reported when the dispatcher names none" (Pepinsky, 1976: 37). The patrol officer, however, did not necessarily record a crime when the dispatcher named one. For example, of 14 assault calls received, reports were filed only in 5 cases. Pepinsky conjectures that reasons for not reporting these incidents are practical ones. That is, as officers had not witnessed the assault and as assault complainants often do not follow through with a formal complaint, the filing of a report probably would not result in an arrest.

A number of other factors affect patrol officers' recording of crimes.[4] For example, Maxfield et al. (1980) found that the ratio of verified crimes to calls for service in which police were dispatched was negatively related to the total demand for police services. They label this phenomenon "load shedding." Interestingly, they find no evidence that this ratio is related to the percentage of blacks or to median family income in the 74 community areas of Chicago that were investigated. Load shedding does not occur for Part I personal crimes; only for Part I property crimes and Part II crimes. That is, it does not occur for the most serious crimes. In a similar vein, others have argued that increases in the number of police per 1000 citizens should increase the rate at which crimes are recorded. It could have the opposite effect, however, if more crimes were thus unfounded.

Although the factors affecting the reporting and recording of crimes have been grouped under different headings, these factors are not necessarily independent. For example, the seriousness of a crime affects not only whether it is reported but also whether it is recorded by the police. Homicides are very likely to be reported by those who discover a victim and are almost always recorded by the police. A shoving match may or may not be reported by the participants or a witness as an assault and those reported may or may not end up in police records. As another example, police recording practices may influence citizen reporting; that is, the perception that the police will not formally follow through on a complaint may discourage citizens from reporting certain crimes.[5]

An interesting summary of the way victim-perceived criminal incidents are translated into crimes known to the police is provided by

Block and Block (1980). By using NCS estimates of victimization, reported victimizations, and the official records of the Chicago Police Department on both founded and unfounded robberies, they estimated that for 50% of the 63,046 cases in which NCS victims of personal robbery said they were victimized, they also said they did not report this victimization to the police. This left an estimated 31,523 cases for which citizens said they had notified the police of a personal robbery. Of these, 73% (23,012) appeared in the initial records of the Chicago Police Department. When these 23,012 incidents were investigated, 18,179 (79%) were founded by the police and thus became part of the *UCR* statistics. This screening process resulted in only 29% of the perceived victimizations being recorded as crimes known to the police. An important additional finding was that when the data were analyzed by the age, sex, and race of the victim, there was no differential filtering of the cases from one stage to the next. Decisions to keep the incident in the flow toward an official report were influenced by the seriousness of the incident, whether the robbery was completed, and whether a gun was used.

We have discussed many of the factors that influence whether incidents will be reported to the police, whether calls to the police will result in an initial record written by the patrol officer who investigates the incident and classifies the crime, and, finally, whether the detective division decides that the evidence shows that the incident was, in fact, a crime in that category.

SOME REASONABLE USES OF *UCR* DATA

After reviewing how *UCR* data are gathered, the types of information that are included and excluded from the *UCR*s, and some of the problems with the data in these reports, we are now in a position to ask about reasonable uses for these data. As we do this, it is important to distinguish among different types of crimes, since the quality of the data contained in the *UCR*s varies by the type of crime under consideration.

First, it is uncontestable that *UCR* rates for most crimes are not an accurate indication of the absolute amount of crime. There are underreporting by citizens, pressures to get crime rates down, police crackdowns, police enforcement styles that encourage informal order maintenance, load shedding, and so on. However, there is reason to suspect that the absolute number of homicides is well reported in official records. This makes sense intuitively and has been supported in studies comparing *UCR* homicide rates with those of the Center for Health Statistics, which publishes data on the causes of death in the United States based on death certificates (Hindelang, 1974). There is also some evidence that the number of motor vehicle thefts recorded in the *UCR*s is close to the number reported by citizens to interviewers in the NCS (see Chapter 5). However, for all other Part I crimes there is substantially less crime recorded than actually occurs.

Second, although the temptation is strong enough to overwhelm many researchers, *UCR* crime rates should not, in general, be used to compare the relative rate of crimes across jurisdictions (for exceptions, see Chapters 5 and 6). We have seen that laws vary from state to state, that pressures on law enforcement agencies to get the crime rate up or down vary from agency to agency, that the style of enforcement varies, that the number of police per capita and their degree of professionalism varies, and so on. There is solid empirical evidence that these factors greatly affect the rates at which crimes are recorded from one jurisdiction to another. The implication is that differences in recorded crime rates are due, to a large extent, to differences in these factors and not only to differences in the rate at which crimes are committed. Inciardi (1978) points to some of the inconsistencies in recorded rates that result from these factors. For example, homicide rates in Colorado and West Virginia are almost identical, yet other violent crime rates in West Virginia are only one-third of those in Colorado. He notes that "North Dakota and South Dakota are geographically and demographically contiguous areas, and have similar rates of total crime, property crimes, and homicide, yet South Dakota's rape and assault rates are three times higher than those of North Dakota" (1978: 7).

Thus, ranking states by their *UCR* crime rates may not shed much light on the relative rate of offending behavior among states. Furthermore, statistical analyses based on the relative rates of crimes for cities (SMSA, states, and so on) may not yield meaningful results. (I will modify these conclusions somewhat after comparing *UCR* and NCS crime rates in Chapter 5.) For instance, the correlation between assault rates (based on *UCR* data) and the number of police per 1,000 residents is likely to reflect either "noise" or some other relationship than that between actual rates of offending behavior and the number of police per capita. It is only fair to note that in *Crime in the United States* the FBI cautions against using these data to make comparisons across jurisdictions.

It has been suggested that *UCR* crime statistics may be used to examine the trend in crime rates within a single jurisdiction, as at least there the laws and practices of the police are the same. Several of the studies cited above, however, indicate that changes in police practices are likely to influence rates within a single jurisdiction. DeFleur (1975) concluded that it was not possible to study changes in the rates and locations of offending within a single city (Chicago) over time due to the impact of changes in police enforcement policies and the number of officers assigned to drug law enforcement. The study by McCleary et al. (1982) of three separate police departments showed marked changes in reported crimes due to organization changes within the departments themselves. Similar results are reported by Selke and Pepinski (1982) and Seidman and Couzens (1974). Thus, it is not, in general, safe to consider changes in official crime rates over time as changes in rates of offending. If one wanted to do so, it would be essential to know of any changes in the department, its political climate, and policies in order to take into account the influence of these variables on official crime rate trends.

Again, it is important to emphasize that the homicide rate probably is an exception. Trends in homicides within the United States and differences in homicide rates between jurisdictions (given a large base population so that rates are not unstable) are probably valid.

There is evidence (see Chapter 5) that the relative rates of offending by offender characteristics such as sex, age, and race are fairly accurate (Hindelang, 1978, 1979, 1981; Hindelang et al., 1979). That is, the preponderance of male over female offenders, blacks over whites, and young over old that is reflected in official statistics is not due solely to criminal justice system bias. These differences in offending rates are reflected (for Part I crimes) in victim reports on surveys and in the self-reports of offenders. This conclusion also is supported by several of the studies cited above that indicate little or no overrecording on the basis of sex or race, and certainly not enough to account for the large differences in the relative offense rates of these groups found in official statistics.

A final use of official statistics is for making local decisions on staffing. Here, local police organizations know how their own data are produced, understand the relationship between stepped-up enforcement and increased rates, and so on. They probably know better than others which areas are high in offense rates for at least Part I offenses. They may also, however, use official data on crime rates for justifying policy decisions that they perceive as in their own interests or that fit their own values.

SUMMARY

A key to understanding many of the strengths and weaknesses of data reported in the *UCR*s, as well as some of their potential uses, is to focus on how these data are produced (Kitsuse and Cicourel, 1963). Crimes officially known to the police include only those crimes that are reported to them or those that they themselves discover. Even those crimes that come to the attention of the police may not be officially recorded as police have a great deal of discretion with respect to how they handle complaints. The reporting behaviors of citizens and the recording behaviors of police are not completely idiosyncratic. Whether a crime is reported to the police depends on factors such as the seriousness of the incident, the relationship of the victim to the offender, and the expectation that the police can do something about the incident. The recording of crimes by the police also depends on a number of factors, such as organizational pressures to keep the crime rate up or down, the seriousness of the offense, the relationship of the victim to the offender, and the wishes of the complainant.

UCR data are gathered and recorded by local law enforcement agencies and reported in aggregate form through the Uniform Crime Reporting Program. The data reported do not include information on the victims of crimes (except for homicide) and do not include data on offender characteristics until the stage of arrest. All of these factors place limits on the usefulness of *UCR* data for social science research and for making policy decisions. Furthermore, the quality of *UCR* data varies depending on the crime. For example, data on homicides and motor vehicle thefts are certainly better than the data on assaults and rapes.

DISCUSSION QUESTIONS

1. The *UCR*s do not collect data on the characteristics of the victims of crime (with the exception of homicide). If such data were collected by the Uniform Crime Reporting Program, how might it be used by policy-makers and social researchers?

2. Why might the victims of Part I crimes not report them to the police? Do not limit yourself to the reasons outlined in this chapter.

3. Why might police officers not officially record a Part I crime incident? Do not limit yourself to the reasons outlined in this chapter.

4. How might the factors that you discussed in Questions 2 and 3 affect the comparison of crime rates across police jurisdictions?

NOTES

1. Skogan (1984) has written an excellent review of worldwide research on the factors affecting the reporting of crimes to police. He lists crime seriousness, victim insurance, feelings of obligation and efficacy, and personal relationships with offenders as major factors in determining crime reporting. Interestingly, he concludes that attitudes toward the police and the personal attributes of victims (sex and race) are relatively independent of crime reporting.

2. Black (1980) has summarized and expanded on these studies in *The Manner and Customs of the Police*.

3. A multivariate analysis of the factors involved in police decisions to arrest suspects or report crimes using data collected by Black and Reiss (1970) was conducted by Friedrich (1977). This unpublished study is summarized by Sherman (1980: 92-93), who found that for arrest decisions legal seriousness was the most powerful predictor, whereas the effects of a suspect's race, class, demeanor, and visibility are negligible. The complainant's preference for arrest and the number of officers present are significantly related to the arrest decision. For decisions to record crimes seriousness is negligible, but citizens' demeanor, race, class, and visibility are significant, whereas complainant preference becomes the most powerful predictor.

4. Sherman's (1980) review of police behavior is perhaps the most comprehensive available; for instance, under individual explanations (officer characteristics) he reviews studies dealing with officer age, sex, education, race, height, length of service, job satisfaction, and racial attitudes. This is just one of four general categories he lists that may affect police behavior; the others are situational, organizational, and community explanations.

5. Black's (1973, 1976) theory of the mobilization of law pertains to both the reporting behavior of citizens and the recording behavior of officers. In addition to many of the factors outlined in this chapter, he suggests that law is more likely to be mobilized by those of higher rank against those of lower rank than vice versa in situations in which other forms of social control are largely absent, and so on. The empirical support for parts of his provocative and insightful theory is the subject of some debate. For an interesting exchange, see Gottfredson and Hindelang (1979a, 1979b) and Black (1979).

3

NATIONAL CRIME SURVEYS:
Victim Reports

Problems with the crime data presented in official reports served to motivate victimization surveys. It was expected that such surveys would provide more reliable measures of the absolute rates of serious crimes and more reliable series on which to base analyses of crime trends in the United States. In addition to data on the rates of offenses, it was envisioned that these surveys would supply more detailed information on a number of situational factors, such as the locations at which crimes occur (home, office, or school), the time of day they occur, whether a weapon was used, and how many offenders and victims were involved. In addition, victims can sometimes identify offender characteristics, such as the sex, race, and age of the offender, as well as the relationship of the offender to the victim. Finally, data from victimization surveys provide information on victims that is not available for most crimes recorded in the *UCR*s: for example, data describing the sex, race, and age of victims, their educational background, marital status, whether they were injured, the amount of medical expenses incurred, whether property that was lost was insured, and several other items.

Although there have been a number of victimization surveys conducted in the United States (see Chapter 1 for a review), I will concentrate on the National Crime Survey (NCS) initiated by the Law Enforcement Assistance Administration and the U.S. Census Bureau. These surveys involve large samples of both households and business establishments. Interviews are conducted with knowledgeable respondents from the sample households or businesses and a series of questions are asked concerning victimizations that may have occurred to members of the household or to the business.

THE COLLECTION OF NCS DATA[1]

The NCSs can be conveniently divided into two separate major programs. The first of these programs involved surveys of cities conducted between 1972 and 1975 and the second is an ongoing national survey that has been conducted continuously since July of 1972.

The City Samples

The city surveys were conducted in 26 large central cities. Thirteen of the cities were surveyed twice and 13 only once. Eight of the cities were surveyed in 1972, 5 in 1973, 13 in 1974, and then the 13 cities surveyed in 1972-1973 were resurveyed in 1975. In these studies a stratified probability sample of about 10,000 households containing 22,000 eligible respondents of age 12 or older was selected. A probability sample (a real sample) of businesses in each city was also selected with (depending on the size of the city) from 1,000 to 5,000 businesses in the sample.

In this way, for each city, estimates of the number of household crimes—household burglary, household larceny, and motor vehicle theft—commercial crimes—commercial burglary and commercial robbery—as well as personal crimes—robbery, rape, simple assault, aggravated assault, and larceny—were obtained. These data can be used to estimate crime incidence rates for these cities and may be compared to the citywide crime rates reported in the *UCRs*.

The city surveys were discontinued in 1975 and have not been resumed. They provide the only source of data on a large number of U.S. cities that may be used to compare survey-generated victimization rates with officially generated crime rates. Such comparisons, however, are limited by a number of factors (discussed in Chapter 5), including the fact that only 26 cities were surveyed and that the reference periods (the period of time for which respondents were asked to remember incidents) differed for these cities. Table 3.1 shows the various cities surveyed, the time of the survey, and the reference period. In each case respondents were asked to report incidents that occurred during a 12-month reference period.

TABLE 3.1
Cities Surveyed and Reference Periods Used
in the NCS City Surveys

Time of Surveys	Cities Surveyed	Reference Period
July 1972	Atlanta, Baltimore, Cleveland, Dallas, Denver, Newark,	July 1971 - Oct. 1972
Nov. 1972	Portland, St. Louis	
January 1973	Chicago, Detroit, Los Angeles,	Jan. 1972 - Feb. 1973
March 1973	New York, Philadelphia	
January 1974	Boston, Buffalo, Cincinnati, Houston, Miami, Milwaukee, Minneapolis, New Orleans, Oakland, Pittsburgh, San Diego,	Jan. 1973-Feb. 1974
March 1974	San Francisco, Washington, D.C.	
January 1975	Chicago, Detroit, Los Angeles,	Jan. 1974 - Feb. 1975
March 1975	New York, Philadelphia	
May 1975	Atlanta, Baltimore, Cleveland, Dallas, Denver, Newark, Portland, St. Louis	Mar. 1974 - Apr. 1975

SOURCE: *An Introduction to the National Crime Survey* (Garafalo and Hindelang, 1977: 16, Figure 1).
NOTE: The reference period was 12 months for each respondent beginning in the month prior to the month in which the interview was conducted. Because the interviews occurred over a period of several months, the reference periods for respondents in each group of cities do not correspond exactly.

The National Sample

The national sample, like the city sample, was originally based on probability samples of both businesses and households (albeit the sampling procedure was more complex). The household surveys began in July of 1972 and continue to date. They currently sample about 60,000 households containing about 136,000 individuals. The sample of businesses was begun in July of 1972 but was discontinued in 1976. While the business surveys were being conducted they included about 50,000 businesses. The sample design involves a panel, in which interviews are conducted in each household at six-month intervals. The interviewer inquires about criminal incidents that may have occurred during the preceding six months. The sample consists of addresses so that a particular address is visited every six months for a maximum of three years, at which time a new address (household) is selected. The panel design helps to provide a "bounded" period (after the first interview) in which the respondent is asked about victimizations occurring since the last interview.

In the household portion of the NCS a knowledgeable adult is designated to answer background questions about the household (e.g., family income, number of household members, and whether the family owns or rents the living unit). The household respondent also answers a series of questions about victimizations that may have occurred in the household—burglary, motor vehicle theft, and larceny from the household premises. Each member of the household 14 years of age or older is interviewed about personal victimizations that may have occurred to them. Proxy interviews are conducted with knowledgeable adults concerning victimizations that may have occurred involving household members who are 12 or 13 years old or those too ill to be interviwed or who are away from the household temporarily and will not return during the period in which the interviews are being conducted. In the city surveys the reference period is for crimes occurring during the past year, in the national surveys the reference period is for crimes occurring during the past six months. Additional background information on all household members (e.g., age, sex, and education) is obtained.

In the business portion of the national survey (that was discontinued in 1976) a person knowledgeable about the business was identified. This person answered a series of background questions about the establishment (e.g., annual income, length of time the business had been located at the current address, and the number of paid employees). The business respondent then answered questions concerning any burglaries or robberies that the business might have suffered during the reference period.

One part of the interview schedules of both the household and business surveys contains a series of "screen" questions designed to elicit information about whether a victimization of any kind occurred. These screen questions are followed by more detailed questions concerning any incidents reported by the respondent. Examples of household screen questions appear in Figure 3.1. The household screen questions are answered by a knowledgeable adult responding for the entire household, and the individual screen questions are asked of all members of the household who are 14 years of age or older. For those household members who are either 12 or 13, a knowledgeable adult answers the individual screen questions. After the screen questions, interviewers ask a series of questions designed to obtain detailed information about any incidents noted in the screen questions (e.g., where the incident occurred, when it occurred, was a weapon used, and so on). The use of screen questions involving each household member rather than only the head of the household resulted from pretest findings that indicated that direct personal interviews with each household member produced over two times as many incident reports for some personal crimes than if only a knowledgeable adult was asked to report crimes for the entire household (Kalish, 1974). The screen questions themselves are used to prevent respondent fatigue. It was found that respondents who had to immediately go through a long report for each incident reported on the screen questions were more likely to not answer that they had been victimized on later screen questions. Biderman et al. (1967) found that the use of screen questions before answering incident reports resulted in two and one-half times more incidents being reported than a procedure that required respondents to answer incident reports immediately after each screen question.

In terms of response rates, the surveys have been quite successful. For the 13 cities surveyed in 1975, at least one interview was conducted in 96% of the housing units selected and in 99% of these households all of the eligible individual respondents were interviewed. The rate of response among businesses surveyed was about 98%. These rates are similar to those for the national survey. Adjustments were made in both the city and national surveys for nonresponding households and businesses. In the national household survey, for example, adjustments are based on the geographic area of residence and the race of the household head. For the business portion of the national survey, adjustments were based on the type of business and its geographic location. These adjustments were made by increasing the weights given to cases that were similar (e.g., same type of business and same geographic area) to the noninterviewed cases.

The classification of crimes in NCS publications follows closely the definitions in the *Uniform Crime Reporting Handbook* (1980) that is used by law enforcement agencies as a guide to classifying crimes for reports that are sent to the FBI (or the state UCR programs where those exist). Two types of counts are made from the data derived from the surveys: a count of criminal incidents and one of victimizations. Incident counts correspond to *UCR* crime counts; that is, only one incident is counted for a continuous sequence of criminal behavior. For example, "if a robber enters a bar and robs the cash register receipts and a wallet from the bartender and personal property from five patrons, the

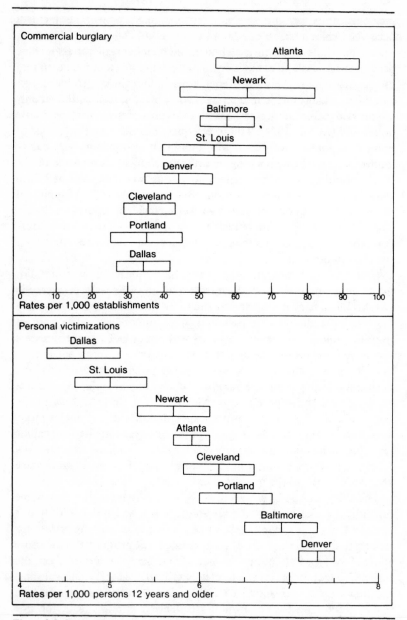

Figure 3.2 Survey Estimates of Crime Rates and Their Confidence Intervals

A major goal of the NCS is to supply detailed data on victimizations; however, there are times when a respondent may have been the victim of what are labeled "series victimizations." This label is applied to victimizations if the incidents are very similar in detail, there are at least three incidents in the series, and the respondent is not able to recall dates and other details well enough to report them. For example, a woman who is abused by her ex-husband on a number of occasions during the six-month reference period may not be able to recall the details or dates of each incident. In most published reports, series victimizations are excluded from the personal and household victimization and incidence counts (rates). Reiss (1978) reports that including series incidents would increase the estimated number of crimes in the United States by about 18%.

WHAT NCS DATA INCLUDE

The types of crimes included in the NCSs are more limited than those covered in the *UCR*s. The NCS screen questions concern only Part I *UCR* crimes (with the exclusion of homicide and arson and the addition of simple assault). Table 3.2 is based on data from the city survey conducted in Boston in 1974 (U.S. Department of Justice, 1975: 17-18). This table indicates the types of crimes covered in the NCS. Furthermore, as noted before, in the NCS a distinction is made between the estimated number of criminal incidents and the estimated number of victims. The reason for this distinction is that a single incident may involve multiple victims. Thus, a sample survey technique that is based on victim reports of criminal incidents is likely to lead to an overestimation of the number of such incidents as each victim can report the single incident. Based on the number of multiple victim incidents reported to NCS interviewers, estimates have been made of both the number of victimizations and the number of incidents. As mentioned above, the number of victims and incidents for household crimes and commercial crimes are the same, because in these cases the household or commercial establishment is considered the victim.

Data from the city surveys were published in a series of reports that combined data from the 13 cities surveyed in 1974, *Criminal Victimization in 13 American Cities* (U.S. Department of Justice, 1975), and 13 cities that were surveyed in 1972 and again in 1975, *Criminal Victimization in Eight American Cities* (U.S. Department of Justice, 1976a)

TABLE 3.2
Personal Crimes: Number of Incidents and Victimizations and
Ratio of Incidents to Victimizations by Type of Crime

Type of Crime	Incidents	Victimizations	Ratio
CRIMES OF VIOLENCE	24,800	29,700	1:1.20
Rape	800	800	1:1.06
Robbery	11,300	13,600	1:1.21
Robbery and attempted robbery with injury	3,400	3,900	1:1.15
from serious assault	1,800	2,200	1:1.21
from minor assault	1,600	1,800	1:1.09
Robbery with injury	4,300	5,600	1:1.29
Attempted robbery without injury	3,500	4,100	1:1.16
Assault	12,800	15,300	1:1.20
Aggravated assault	5,900	7,400	1:1.25
with injury	2,200	2,700	1:1.21
attempted assault with weapon	3,700	4,700	1:1.27
Simple assault	6,900	7,900	1:1.15
with injury	1,800	2,100	1:1.16
attempted assault without weapon	5,100	5,800	1:1.15
CRIMES OF THEFT	50,600	52,500	1:1.04
Personal larceny with contact	10,900	11,600	1:1.06
Purse snatching	2,300	2,400	1:1.03
Attempted purse snatching	2,100	2,200	1:1.06
Pocket picking	6,500	7,000	1:1.08
Personal larceny without contact	39,700	41,000	1:1.03

SOURCE: Criminal Victimization Surveys in Boston (U.S. Department of Justice, 1977)
NOTE: Details may not add to total shown because of rounding: ratios calculated from unrounded figures. Because of data processing problems, a manual weighting procedure was used for estimating the number of incidents of personal larceny without contact. As it was not feasible to perform an adjustment for cases involving more than one victim, the estimated number of incidents may be slightly inflated.

and *Criminal Victimization in Chicago, Detroit, Los Angeles, New York, Philadelphia* (U.S. Department of Justice, 1976b). These publications provide estimates of the number and rate of victimizations and criminal incidents for each of the crimes in Table 3.2 for each of the 26 cities. Furthermore, they provide estimates of the percentage of victimizations involving strangers and nonstrangers and victimization rates by sex, age, race, and annual family income for personal crimes, and by race, age of head of household, and annual family income for household crimes. For commercial crimes, they estimate rates per 1,000 establishments by type of establishment (retail, wholesale, service, or other), gross annual receipts, and the average number of paid employees. The percentage of victimizations that respondents say they reported to the police are also presented for each type of crime.

More detailed breakdowns of the data are available for the 13 cities surveyed in 1974 in a series of 13 publications (one for each city) available from the Bureau of Justice Statistics. For example, in these publications victimization rates are broken down by the sex of the victim and the perceived sex of the offender, by the perceived race of the offender and the race of the victim, by the perceived age of the offender and the age of the victim, by race and perceived loss or damage (estimated in dollars), and by several other variables. These publications provide a wealth of data on victimizations for the city-level surveys.

Although it is not the focus of this book, the NCS randomly administered a supplemental attitude questionnaire to half of the selected households in each of these 13 cities. These surveys contained questions designed to measure opinions, beliefs, and actual behaviors that are relevant to the issue of crime. The results from these surveys also have been published in a series of 13 reports that are available from the Bureau of Justice Statistics.[2]

Data from the national sample surveys are presented in published form in a series of annual publications by the U.S. Department of Justice entitled *Criminal Victimization in the United States*. These publications have tables similar to those described above, but are, of course, crime estimates for the entire United States. In addition, data on trends from the preceding year (or years) are reported. These tables do not include data broken down by rates of victimization or incidents by geographic areas.

A major advantage of the NCS data is that they are recorded on the individual level for personal crimes, household level for household crime, and business establishment level for commercial crimes. This contrasts with *UCR* data that are aggregated at the level of reporting agencies and are available for public use at the level of cities, counties, SMSAs, and so on. That is, *UCR* data come in highly aggregate form. This makes it possible to generate tables relating, for example, the income level of assault victims by their race and whether or not they had medical coverage or any other tables for which individual questions were asked. Computer tapes are available for this and other purposes through the Interuniversity Consortium for Political and Social Research (ICPSR) and the Data Use and Access Laboratories (DUALabs).[3]

Thus, in many respects the data available from the NCS are more detailed than those available from the *UCR*, not only in terms of information supplied about the situations in which offenses occur, but in terms of details about both the offender and the victim.

WHAT NCS DATA EXCLUDE

A major advantage of the *UCR*s over the NCSs is that the NCS data are based on a sample of U.S. households and businesses. Although these samples are large enough to provide reliable estimates of crime rates for the United States as a whole, or even for males and females in the United States, they are not large enough to provide estimates of crime rates for most states or cities. As a National Academy of Sciences study recently concluded (Penick and Owens, 1976: 144), "it appears unlikely that state-level data can be disaggregated with any detail, because of sampling errors and because of restictions relating to confidentiality requirements." Thus, the *UCR*s are the only data base that provide detailed geographic coverage.

Although the NCSs eliminate one major filter from the crime recording process (i.e., having crimes become officially known to the police), they focus on a far narrower range of crimes than do the *UCR*s. They provide no data on Part II crimes (except for simple assault); thus, crimes such as fraud, embezzlement, forgery, gambling, drug abuse, and so on are not reported. For information on these crimes other sources must be used.

A number of important factors that potentially contribute to victimization and could feasibly be collected in the NCS survey are not. Penick and Owens (1976) mention environmental factors, such as the location of the victimization in relation to the center of town, median income of the community, predominant housing type, and the racial composition and crime rates in the surrounding area. Data on attributes of households, such as daytime occupancy, security practices, and ease of access to the building, and better information on the location of victimizations (e.g., whether an assault occurred at a bar, office, football game, or on public transportation) easily could be collected. All of these could aid our understanding of victimization. They criticize the NCS for being too focused on the description of victimization and not enough concerned with the explanation of victimization.

Although the continuing national surveys are based on a panel design (i.e., seven interviews at six-month intervals over a three-year period), it is not possible to follow individuals from one reference period to the next. If this were possible, it would provide a rich source of data on victim proneness and multiple victimization. In a similar vein, it would be helpful to have some published data on the characteristics of those victimized 0, 1, 2, . . . N times. It is likely that those victimized only a single time differ in systematic ways from those victimized more than once, just as repeat offenders differ from one time offenders.

PROBLEMS WITH NCS DATA

As with *UCR* data, it is helpful to think about NCS crime rates by considering how they are produced. For example, these estimates are based on sample surveys in which respondents answer a series of questions that are posed by an interviewer. As in other interviews, these interviews are social interactions in which the interviewer is asking the respondent for his or her time and effort. The interview may be perceived as boring, stupid, or threatening. Furthermore, interviewers may have little or nothing to offer respondents in return for their time. The data that result from these interviews share many of the weaknesses of data gathered in other sample survey interviews (e.g., sampling errors, social desirability responses, forgetting about past events, and so on). Fortunately, several studies have been conducted that estimate the effects of several of these and other factors on the crime rate estimates produced by the NCSs.

A large number of studies have examined the accuracy of respondent reports of criminal incidents. One technique involves "reverse record checks" in which police records are searched for crimes that have been recorded and then the victims of these crimes are interviewed using the standard NCS method. The question is, how many respondents will recall (or report) crimes to the interviewer that are recorded in the police records?

In one study, Turner (1972) investigated 206 cases of robbery, assault, and rape from police records; it was found that only 63.1% of these incidents were reported to the interviewer. Not surprisingly, the percentage reporting these incidents to interviewers was strongly related to the relationship of the offender and the victim. When the offender was a stranger (N = 99) 76.3% of the incidents were reported to the interviewer, when the offender was known to the victim (N = 78) 56.9% of the incidents were reported, and when the offender was a relative (N = 18) only 22.2% of the incidents were reported. In a similar study in Baltimore (Murphy and Dodge, 1981), only 36.7% of the assaults, 75% of the larcenies, 76% of the robberies, and 86% of the burglaries were reported. Personal crimes of violence (especially assaults) that have been recorded in police records are especially unlikely to be reported to interviewers. One may speculate about why this is so; for example, whom is the victim and whom the offender in some assaults may be difficult to determine (that is, the victim may be, or be afraid to appear, partly culpable). The fact that assaults often may involve people whom the victim knows may make reporting such incidents to interviewers embarrassing and/or painful. Victims may fear reprisal from the offender if the offender somehow discovers their report to the interviewer.

A second type of record check has been conducted—"forward record checks." Here, crimes that respondents claim to have reported to the police are the focus of study. A search of police records is conducted attempting to locate these incidents. The sole study of this type was conducted in Portland, Oregon by Schneider (1977). She used crimes that respondents said they had reported to the police in the 1974 city survey in Portland. After an exhaustive search of police records, she found that 45% of the crimes were definitely in the records. She was unable to find any record for 34% of the crimes said to have been reported to the police. In the remaining 21% of the cases, the original location of the incident was too vague (16%), the victim report and police records were in disagreement concerning the incident that occurred (4%), or the event was found in police records, but a crime report on the incident was not filed by the police (1%).

In both the forward and reverse record checks, it is possible to ascertain the degree to which survey techniques of classifying the incidents agree with police classification of the incidents. For the 212 cases in the Portland study with a definite match in police records, 91% of the incidents were classified in the same category by the police and the respondents (rape, robbery, assault, burglary, larceny, and auto theft). The greatest difference in classification was for personal crimes. These results are somewhat similar to those reported in the San Jose (reverse record check) study. In that study (Turner, 1972), 97% of the burglaries were classified in the same category in both the survey and police records. The percentage agreement was 85% for personal offenses and 82% for larcenies.

Not all of the nonreporting of crimes to interviewers can be attributed to respondent embarrassment about the incident or other "protective" mechanisms. Part of it is due to memory decay or forgetting. In the San Jose reverse record study, Turner (1972) found a relationship between the number of months between the reported incident and the interview and the percentage of incidents that were reported to the interviewer. For those incidents occurring 1 to 3 months before the interview, 69% were recalled (N = 101), for those occurring 4 to 6 months before, 50% were recalled (N = 100), for those occurring 7 to 9 months previously, 46% were recalled (N = 103), and only 30% of those occurring 10 to 12 months previously (N = 90) were recalled. Other reverse record check studies (i.e., in Washington, see Dodge, 1970, and Baltimore, see Yost and Dodge, 1970) found a decline in the percentage of incidents recalled as the time between the interview and the recorded incident increased.[4]

A major problem facing the NCS at its inception involved the "telescoping" of events, which is remembering incidents as occurring more recently than they actually occurred (forward telescoping) or as occurring in the more distant past (backward telescoping). This problem is especially troublesome if crime incidents are moved either forward into the reference period for the interviewer (i.e., last 12 months for the city surveys or last 6 months for the national surveys) or backward out of the reference period. In early victimization studies it was found that forward telescoping is more common than backward telescoping and, thus, this factor increased the number of victimization incidents reported in any given reference period. The solution used in the NCS national survey is referred to as a bounded interview. When a household first moves into the national panel and its members are first interviewed, the data serve as a baseline and victimizations reported are not used to estimate national rates. When they are reinterviewed six months later they are asked about incidents that have occurred since the last interview. In addition, the NCS interviewer has a summary list of the victimizations reported during the previous interview. This allows for a filtering out of victimizations occurring in the earlier period from the estimate of the number of incidents occurring in the present period.

As the NCS interviews contain unbounded interviews for new housing units in the sample as well as bounded interviews for those continuing in the panel, it is possible to compare the bounded and unbounded estimates. The unbounded interviews result in estimated victimization rates that are 30% to 40% higher than the bounded interviews (Woltman et al., 1975). This problem is taken into consideration in the continuing national survey by not including the interview data for unbounded households in the victimization estimates. It is important to note that the city-level surveys conducted between 1972 and 1975 were unbounded; however, they did use a 12-month reference period rather than a 6-month period, which may have led to greater forgetting of incidents in the reference period. There is no guarantee that these two effects balanced each other.

NCS estimates of crime rates often involve a substantial amount of sampling error. The problem arises because reports of victimization are relatively rare. For example, estimates for rape victimization in Philadelphia were based on only 29 actual interviews with rape victims and in Detroit only about 150 robbery victims were interviewed in the city surveys (Jacob, 1975). Such low frequencies of events are associated with relatively large confidence intervals. For several of the city surveys, so few rape victims were interviewed that the estimates involving rape broken down by strangers and offenders known to the victim are judged almost completely unreliable. These results occur even though each of the city-level surveys involved 10,000 households (containing roughly 22,000 individuals).

Skogan has graphically portrayed this problem by constructing 95% confidence intervals around estimates of crime rates for both commercial burglaries and personal victimization for the 8 cities involved in the 1972 city surveys. These confidence intervals mark the range in which we can be 95% confident the rate would lie if we had attempted to interview everyone in the city rather than just a sample. As can be seen in Figure 3.2, even when personal victimizations are grouped into a single category (so that they are less rare events), the confidence intervals are quite wide. Furthermore, as Skogan (1981: 3) notes, "cities such as Newark, Baltimore, St. Louis, and Denver have virtually indistinguishable commercial burglary victimization rates despite large differences in their estimated values (63 per 1000 in Newark, 44 per 1000 in Denver), because the large confidence intervals around these figures largely overlap."

In addition to sampling errors, the results of victimization surveys are subject to interviewer effects (Bailey et al., 1978). That is, some interviewers are able to elicit a larger number of reported incidents from respondents than are other interviewers. This may be due to a more probing interview style or the creation of just the right amount of rapport with the respondent or to a different interpretation of the aims of the survey by different interviewers. Whatever the reasons for differences in the victimization rates produced by various interviewers,

29. Now I'd like to ask some questions about crime. They refer only to the last 6 months - between _____ 1, 197_ and _____, 197_. During the last 6 months, did anyone break into or somehow illegally get into your apartment/ home), garage, or another building on your property?

    Yes _____   No _____   How many times? _____

30. (Other than the incident(s) just mentioned) Did you find a door jimmied, a lock forced, or any other signs of an ATTEMPTED break in?

    Yes _____   No _____   How many times? _____

31. Was anything at all stolen that is kept outside your home, or happened to be left out, such as a bicycle, a garden hose, or lawn furniture? (other than any incidents already mentioned)

    Yes _____   No _____   How many times? _____

32. Did anyone take something belonging to you or to any member of this household, from a place where you or they were temporarily staying, such as a friend's or relative's home, a hotel or motel, or a vacation home?

    Yes _____   No _____   How many times? _____

33. What was the total number of motor vehicles (cars, trucks, etc.) owned by you or any other member of this household during the last 6 months?

    0 _____   1 _____   2 _____   3 _____   4 or more _____

34. Did anyone steal, TRY to steal, or use (it/any of them) without permission?

    Yes _____   No _____   How many times? _____

35. Did anyone steal or TRY to steal parts attached to (it/any of them), such as a a battery, hubcaps, tape-deck, etc.?

    Yes _____   No _____   How many times? _____

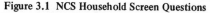

Figure 3.1 NCS Household Screen Questions

UCR counts only one robbery; there was a single incident of robbery in which there were six victimizations" (Garofalo and Hindelang, 1977: 22). In the NCS both incidents and victimizations are counted. For the crimes involving households (household burglary, household larceny, and motor vehicle theft) and businesses (robbery and burglary), there is no distinction between victimizations and incidents as in these cases the household or business is considered to be the victim. For personal crimes, however (e.g., rape, assault, robbery, and personal larceny), the distinction between the number of incidents and the number of persons victimized must be carefully observed. In most NCS publications victimization rates are reported, but sometimes incidence rates are also reported. Of course, the rate of victimization has to be at least equal to the incidence rate.

the effects can be large. For example, in the city survey for Baltimore it is necessary to multiply the estimated sampling variance by 1.60 before calculating the 95% confidence interval. This increases the confidence interval for the victimization rate (for all crimes) from 40-180 per 1,000 to 20-200 per 1,000. The confidence intervals in Figure 3.2 do not take this additional source of error into account.

The size of the interviewer effect decreases as the number of respondents any one person interviews decreases and as the number of interviewers increases. Thus, given the design of the national surveys, this effect should be substantially smaller than in the city surveys. The national surveys, however, are not immune to problems of sampling errors even though they employ a sample of some 60,000 households. Here, it may be possible to estimate accurately victimization rates for the country as a whole, but not for regions or for specific subgroups of the population (e.g., married black females 60 years of age and over).

Another problem related to the sampling design of the NCS is referred to as panel or time in sample bias. The problem is that those who have been interviewed before know that if they answer a screen question positively they will be questioned further about the incident. Therefore, there should be a tendency to report fewer victimizations to interviewers the longer a respondent has been in the panel. Indeed, there is evidence of this effect, but the effect seems to be relatively small. For most crimes, when those interviewed for the second time are compared to those interviewed the seventh (final) time, the differences are less than 10% (Woltman and Bushery, 1975). It has been suggested that these differences might also be due to respondents becoming more careful in avoiding crime after having been interviewed, but there is no direct evidence on this issue. It is noteworthy, however, that respondents who have been in previous waves of the panel are much more likely than first-time respondents to say that they reported crimes to the police (Murphy and Cowan, 1976).

The panel design of the survey presents yet another problem—the mover-stayer problem. The national survey is based on a sample of dwelling units. When a household moves the dwelling unit stays in the sample and the new household is treated as if it has already had a bounding interview. This aspect of the panel design creates two problems. First, the unbounded interview should result in higher reported rates of victimization. The second problem is more complex and involves the fact that movers are different than stayers. For example, Murphy and Cowan (1976) found that replacement households—which make up 10% of all NCS interviews—account for 18% of all victimizations. This may (in part) be because these interviews are not bounded or because movers into the sample are more prone to victimizations. On the other hand, those who move out of the sample are also more likely to have been victimized. For example, Lehnen and Reiss (1978) found that 24% of those households reporting one victimization "disappeared" from the sample six months later, whereas 35% of those households reporting three or more victimizations disappeared. The overall effect of panel bias and attrition is likely to reduce the number of victimizations uncovered by the survey method, whereas the unbounded interviews with those who move into the panel are likely to increase the number of victimizations uncovered.

Two other factors may lower the number of reported victimizations. One factor involves the use of a single household respondent to represent the entire household when assessing household crimes and the other involves the increasing use of telephone interviews in the surveys. It was noted earlier that the use of a single individual to report victimizations for all members of a household leads to far fewer reports of victimization than when each individual in the household is queried about personal crimes. The NCS, however, has only a single respondent answer questions about household crimes (i.e., burglary, household larceny, and motor vehicle theft). This may lead to a substantial undercounting of these events. A study by Dodge (1976) found that 10% of the motor vehicle thefts, 14% of the burglaries, and 31% of the household larcenies were reported by other household members in response to questions that were not designated to stimulate the recall of household crimes. No one knows how many additional household crimes would be reported if each household member were asked about these incidents.

In the NCSs, during the interviewer's first visit, a list of all household members is made and all available respondents are interviewed. For those household members who are not at home, however, a follow-up interview may be conducted by phone. In fact, the proportion of interviews conducted by phone has increased steadily from 25% in 1974 to over 60% in 1980 (Sparks, 1981). There is some evidence, however, that respondents interviewed in person report higher rates of victimization than those interviewed by telephone (Woltman and Bushery, 1978; Turner, 1977). Other researchers, however, have reported that telephone interviewing does not reduce reported victimization rates (Catlin and Murray, 1979; Tuchfarber and Klecka, 1976).

The problems discussed above have focused on underreporting, but a potentially more bothersome problem is a reporting bias linked to education. Sparks (1981: 33), for example, presents data that indicate that the aggravated assault rate for whites with 0-4 years of education is 4.3 per 1,000, whereas it is 8.0 for those with 13-15 years of education. For blacks the comparable figures are 5.1 for 0-4 years and 16.4 for 13-15 years. The same trend is evident for simple assault, for which whites with 0-4 years of education have a rate of 7.2 and those with 13-15 years a rate of 16.0. For blacks, the rate is 2.3 for those with 0-4 years of education and 10.6 for those with 13-15 years. The reasons for the positive relation of victimization with education are not clear. Skogan (1981) suggests that it may be due to differential respondent productivity. The rationale for this suggestion is that more educated respondents are more cooperative and at ease in interview situations and, thus, more able to recall victimizations. After all, the interview situation is not unlike a testing situation. It might also be that individuals with different levels of education have different definitions of assault. Whatever the reason, Skogan (1981: 12) suggests that the results are not to be taken at face value. He states that, "during the early stages of development we often have less confidence in our measures than in our theories, and such findings indicate that further methodological research may be called for." Similarly, Sparks (1981: 34) argues that these results are due to response biases and do not reflect the relationship between education and victimization as it really is: "Between believing such a wild implausibility, and doubting the validity of the survey data, the choice should be clear."

The implications of this type of response bias for social research are serious, as education is highly correlated with individual characteristics such as income, race, age and place of residence. On the city level, at which the median education of cities is positively related to the percentage of whites, low population density, high income, and so on, such a bias can distort substantially research findings. In fact, we find that high rates of interpersonal violence are positively associated with good housing, low population density, high income, and high levels of formal education (Skogan, 1981: 31). We do not know if this is due to a response bias or if our theories are wrong, but both Skogan and Sparks have stated clearly their own views. The potential for method dependent research results, however, is clear.

SOME REASONABLE USES OF NCS DATA

Like *UCR* data, the data collected by the NCSs is limited in both its coverage and its accuracy. In this section I will delineate some potential uses of these data. The first of these involves an estimate of the rate of various crimes.

Most researchers agree that the NCS data reflect fewer victimizations than actually occur. After all, there is panel bias, embarrassment in reporting crimes to interviewers (especially those perpetrated by known offenders), memory decay, the exclusion of series incidents, and so on. An exception to this consensus is Levine (1976), who notes the potential for overreporting in the NCSs. He argues that respondents may feel under pressure to produce crime reports after a series of negative answers on screen questions, that interviewers may feel that they should produce positive results for their employers, and that coders of the data may respond to the same pressures. He also cites a study by Ennis (1967) in which trained evaluators scrutinized the reports of 3,296 cases of reported victimizations and disqualified 34.9% of these events because the facts reported by the alleged victims were not sufficient to define the event as a criminal act. This procedure is akin to the unfounding of crimes reported to the police. Still, most researchers feel that these biases are outweighed by those factors leading to underreporting (Sparks, 1981; Singer, 1978). However, Levine (1976, 1978) mentions another potential problem with victimization rate estimates that is, perhaps, more telling. That is, they may include a number of trivial incidents, ones that were seen by respondents as not important enough to report to the police.

Chambliss (1984) makes a similar argument in an article entitled "Crime Rates and Crime Myths." He notes that 40% of the estimated 37 million victimizations reported in the 1973 NCS were for personal larceny and that 95% of these were personal larcenies without contact. This crime involves theft without direct contact between the victim and offender. It also includes attempted theft. These crimes may involve, for example, the theft of property left in an unlocked desk, on top of a desk, or in an open car. Furthermore, over 60% of the victims of these crimes say that they did not report them to the police. The major reasons given for not reporting were that nothing could be done, that there was a lack of proof, and that it was not important enough. In fact, Chambliss (1984) argues that one of the most useful findings from the NCSs is that, although there appears to be more crime than is reflected in official records, the dark figure of unrecorded crime is not nearly as great as might have been feared. Serious criminal victimization is a rare event. Similarly, Sparks (1981: 17) notes that "in 1977, for example, NCS data show that crimes of violence including robbery occurred at a rate of 33.9 victimizations per 1,000 persons aged 12 and over; about three-quarters of these incidents involved attempts only and did not result in any physical injury." Finally, in any given year, over 90% of the respondents report having not been the victim of any crime, whether attempted, minor, or major.

Another goal of the NCS was to provide information about the characteristics of victims of crime. For instance, what are the relative rates of victimization for males and females; old, middle-aged, and young adults; blacks and whites; and urban and rural residents. Success here depends in large part on the extent of response bias by different groups. There is some evidence of response bias based on education (higher education being associated with greater reporting of victimizations to the NCS interviewers) and some evidence that whites are more likely to report victimizations than are blacks. Further studies are necessary to determine the extent of such biases. In spite of this fact, the NCS remains our major source of data on the characteristics of the victims of crime.

One "victim related characteristic" that is not accurately reflected in the NCSs is the relationship of the victim to the offender. This is seen most dramatically in the reverse record checks. These studies found that a substantially smaller percentage of the incidents recorded in police files were reported to interviewers when the offender was a relative rather than a stranger. Thus, the survey estimates almost certainly underrepresent the proportion of crimes involving relatives. This also reduces the number of victimizations reported for those crimes that often involve family members, such as aggravated and simple assaults.

Given the fact that the NCS is conducted by a single agency and that the interview schedule is the same for respondents in different cities, it was expected that the NCSs would provide comparable data across jurisdictions and could provide a basis for assessing national victimization trends. The surveys probably are more satisfactory for the latter task. In terms of comparing rates across areas (e.g., cities, counties, and SMSAs), the sample size in the national surveys is too small to allow such breakdowns and still have statistically reliable results. Although tabulations of the national data have been made for central cities of SMSAs, the remainder of SMSAs (outside central cities), non-SMSA areas, and the 10 largest states, these data often are not very reliable. Furthermore, some of the most useful information on crime rates from a policy-making point of view is the most local (e.g., precinct-level data). Even the city-level surveys that sampled 10,000 households in each city have problems with statistical reliability (see Figure 3.2). The second problem has to do with response bias. That is, are respondents in some areas more likely to report crimes to NCS interviewers than those in other areas? There is some evidence that this may be the case. If there is an association between education and reporting crimes to the interviewer or between race and the perception of an event as a reportable victimization (as discussed above), those areas with a relatively high percentage of blacks and relatively low education should have relatively low rates of reported victimization. This is, indeed, the case for rates involving violent crimes in the city surveys. Furthermore, the proportion of crimes that respondents say they reported to the police varies greatly from city to city (see Table 5.2). The proportion of victimizations that respondents report to NCS interviewers also may vary from city to city.

The outlook for the measurement of crime trends nationally is more optimistic. Here, one might assume that response bias is relatively constant. That is, that blacks and whites do not change dramatically in their inclination to report crimes to interviewers from year to year. If the proportion of incidents that are reported to (and recorded by) NCS interviewers does not change, the measurement of trends should be possible. Some cautions concerning the use of the NCS survey data to measure trends should be mentioned. The increased use of the telephone interviews from 25% in 1974 to 60% in 1980 might affect the number of reported incidents. Furthermore, until 1975 the household respondent could be any member of the household over the age of 14; since that time the person is required to be at least 18, unless the head of the household or spouse is under that age.

Despite these problems, the NCS survey data have provided us with a rich source of data on victimization. They have helped provide a sense of the size of the dark figure of unreported crime and have provided some sense of the rate of victimization suffered by various groups; for example, although the aged are more fearful of crime than other age groups, they report fewer victimizations (O'Brien et al., 1982). The surveys contain information on the places in which people are victimized. The finding from previous studies that personal crimes tend to be intraracial has been supported by NCS data. In fact, as we shall see in

Chapter 5, the relative rates of offending by males and females, blacks and whites, and old and young found in the NCSs are remarkably similar to those found in the *UCR*s. All of these results are from a data set that has only begun to be tapped. The surveys themselves are undergoing research in preparation for redesign under the direction of Albert Biderman. There is reason to hope that the quality of the data they produce will be improved.

SUMMARY

The NCSs have involved three sets of related studies: a series of methodological surveys; surveys of 26 large American cities; and a continuing national survey. The NCSs have several potential advantages over the *UCR*s: they allow for the collection of data on the victims of crime; they gather data on the individual, household, and business level; and they are "closer" to the actual incident than the data collected by the *UCR*s as they do not depend on police reporting behavior and, thus, have fewer filters. Because NCS data are based on sample surveys, however, a number of problems inherent in this technique make some of the data derived from the NCSs problematic; for example, the reporting behavior of respondents and sampling and interviewer errors. Fortunately, several methodological studies have been conducted using victimization survey techniques and these have helped delineate the scope of many of these problems and helped provide "solutions" to some of them (e.g., bounding interviews, the use of screen questions, and the specification of a six-month reference period). Two major problems that have not been solved involve the reporting of crimes of personal violence (aggravated assault, simple assault, and rape) and, more generally, the reporting of crimes involving relatives and friends, and how to handle the large number of series victimizations.

The data in the NCSs are collected on individual, household, and business levels, which allows greater flexibility in their use than is possible using *UCR* data. Except for the city-level surveys that were discontinued in 1975, however, there is no victimization data that can be used to study city-level units of analysis. Consequently, NCS data allow for analyses at the individual, household, and business levels with only limited analysis across geographic areas, whereas the *UCR* data allow for analyses involving geographic areas but not individual-level analyses. The NCSs have added to our store of knowledge about criminal activities and victimization; they have provided a glimpse of the dark figure of unreported crime, provided information on victims (as opposed to offenders), suggested why victims don't always report crimes to the police, and provided an alternative source of information about offenders.

DISCUSSION QUESTIONS

1. Imagine the crimes of rape and burglary. Why might the victims of these crimes be reticent to report their victimizations to NCS interviewers?

2. Discuss the specific factors involving the way in which NCS data are collected that may result in an underestimation of victimization rates.

3. Discuss the specific factors involving the way in which NCS data are collected that may lead to an overestimation of victimization rates.

4. Discuss how the problem of series victimization affects estimates of the absolute rate of victimization. If the problem of series victimizations were to affect the relative rates of victimization for various cities (e.g., the ranking of cities in terms of the aggravated assault rate), what special sort of bias would be necessary?

NOTES

1. Several excellent publications outlining victimization survey designs and problems associated with them are available (see, especially, Garofalo and Hindelang, 1977; Lehnen and Skogan, 1981; Skogan, 1981; Sparks, 1981). I have used these and other sources extensively in developing this chapter.

2. These reports are entitled *Criminal Victimization Surveys in* [name of city]: *A National Crime Survey Report.* They are published by the National Criminal Justice Information and Statistics Service, Law Enforcement Assistance Administration, U.S. Department of Justice, Washington, D.C.

3. The address for ICPSR is: P.O. Box 1248, Ann Arbor, MI, and for DUALabs Incorporated: 1601 North Kent Street, Arlington, VA.

4. These memoranda (Dodge, 1970; Yost and Dodge, 1970) are cited in Skogan, 1981.

4

SELF-REPORT SURVEYS:
Offender Reports

The third major method for gathering data on crime is the self-report (SR) method. This method does not involve examining police records or asking the victims of crime about criminal incidents; instead it involves asking the offenders themselves, or at least samples of respondents, about behavior that may lead to their classification as offenders.

Chronologically, SR studies came after the development of the Uniform Crime Reporting system and before the NCSs. Although there were some isolated SR surveys in the 1940s (Porterfield, 1946; Wallerstein and Wyle, 1947), the technique gained popularity with the work of Short and Nye (1957, 1958). They showed conclusively that people would admit to delinquent behavior on a questionnaire and, indeed, admit to much more delinquency than was evident from official records. Since their studies, the SR method has been the dominant source of data for articles concerned with the etiology of criminal behavior. Some prominent SR studies are the following: Akers, 1964; Clark and Tifft, 1966; Dentler and Monroe, 1961; Elliott and Voss, 1974; Elliott et al., 1983; Erickson and Empey, 1963; Farrington, 1973; Gold, 1966, 1970; Gold and Reimer, 1975; Gould, 1969; Hardt and Peterson-Hardt, 1977; Hindelang, 1973; Hindelang et al., 1981; Hirschi, 1969; Petersilia, 1978; Shapland, 1978; Voss, 1963; Waldo and Chiricos, 1972; Williams and Gold, 1972.

Unlike the *UCRs* and the NCSs, there is no single set of crimes investigated or single design by which SR data are gathered. Different researchers have used diverse sets of questions and sampled different populations. In this discussion, I will examine three studies in some detail. The Short and Nye studies (1957, 1958), the National Youth Survey (Elliott et al., 1983) and a methodological study of SR methods conducted by Hindelang et al. (1981). The first of these studies is examined because of its historical interest and its influence on the studies that followed; the National Youth Survey (NYS), because it is based on a national panel and is the most comprehensive SR study to date; and the Seattle methods study because of the answers it provides concerning some of the strengths and weaknesses of the SR method.

THE COLLECTION OF SR DATA

As mentioned above, SR studies differ on a number of dimensions. One of these is whether a questionnaire or an interview is used to collect data on self-reported offenses. Short and Nye's original studies involved the use of questionnaires to ascertain levels of delinquency. They presented a checklist of behaviors to respondents (see Table 4.1) and collected other relevant data, such as sex of respondent, whether the respondent was from a broken home, and the SES of the home from which the respondent came. The ongoing National Youth Survey (NYS) uses a face-to-face interview to ascertain self-reported delinquency. Another data collection technique involves the use of "lie detectors" to encourage honest answers to delinquency questions and to evaluate the honesty of responses (see Clark and Tifft, 1966; Hindelang et al., 1981). One might argue for either interviews or questionnaires in terms of providing more accurate data and some evidence on this question is reviewed later.

Another dimension on which SR studies have differed is sampling design. A typical design involves the sampling of a school population and of an institutionalized population or a population with known police records. For example, Short and Nye (1958) sampled high school students in three western high schools, took a 100% sample of students in three midwestern high schools, and a sample from a western training school. The Seattle methods study (Hindelang et al., 1981) sampled three separate groups in order to maximize the variance on delinquency and to represent the general adolescent population of Seattle. One sample was of students enrolled in Seattle public schools for the 1977-1978 academic year, another from those with a record of contact with the Seattle police but with no recorded juvenile court record, and the third from the population of adolescents referred to the juvenile court serving Seattle. These studies are designed to contrast different populations, but are not designed to be generalized to larger populations of cities or regions of the country.

TABLE 4.1
The Short and Nye Self-Report Delinquency Items

Recent research has found that everyone breaks some rules and regulations during his lifetime. Some break them regularly, others less often. Below are some frequently broken. Check those that you have broken since beginning grade school.

1. Driven a car without a driver's license or permit? (Do not include driver training.)
   (1) very often _____ (2) several times_____ (3) once or twice _____ (4) no_____

2. Skipped school without a legitimate excuse?
   (1) no _____ (2) once or twice _____ (3) several times_____ (4) very often_____

3. Defied your parents' authority (to their face)?
   (1) no_____ (2) once or twice _____ (3) several times_____ · (4) very often _____

4. Taken little things (worth less than $2) that did not belong to you?
   (1) no_____ (2) once or twice_____ (3) several times _____ (4) very often_____

5. Bought or drank beer, wine, or liquor? (Include drinking at home.)
   (1) no _____ (2) once or twice_____ (3) several times_____ (4) very often_____

6. Purposely damaged or destroyed public or private property that did not belong to you?
   (1) very often _____ (2) once or twice_____ (3) several times_____(4) no_____

7. Had sex relations with a person of the opposite sex? (1) no _____
   (2) once or twice _____ (3) three or four times _____ (4) five or six times _____
   (5) seven or eight times _____ (6) nine times or more_____

SOURCE: Nye (1958: 13-14). These seven items comprise their final scale.

There have been only two national surveys devoted to self-reported delinquency. The National Surveys of Youth conducted in 1967 and 1972 (Gold, 1970; Gold and Reimer, 1975; Williams and Gold, 1972) and the NYS that followed a panel of respondents from 1976 through 1980 (Elliott et al., 1983). The sampling designs of national surveys can be quite complex. The NYS, for example, employed a multistage cluster probability sample of households in the continental United States.

WHAT SR DATA INCLUDE

The SR method is the dominant method in criminology for studying the etiology of crime. It is suited ideally for this task, as it allows the researcher an opportunity to collect detailed information about individual "offenders." This is in marked contrast to both *UCR* and NCS data. Victimization surveys provide little information about offenders;

for personal crimes it is sometimes possible for the victim to report the race, sex and approximate age of the offender; some additional data are available on the relationship of the offender to the victim. *UCR* data include information on offender characteristics only for those arrested and then for only on a few demographic characteristics (e.g., sex, race, and age). For some crimes, (e.g., homicide) data also are available on the relationship of the offender to the victim. Furthermore, these data are compiled on an aggregate rather than an individual level, making them inappropriate for the study of the etiology of criminal behavior on an individual level. It is true, however, that official crime records may be used by researchers to study individual offenders (e.g., Wolfgang, 1958; Pokorny, 1965; Pittman and Handy, 1964; Amir, 1967). Even when compared to these searches of official records, SR studies potentially offer much fuller information on offenders.

The type of information on the offender (family background, demographic characteristics, personality measures, etc.) that is included in SR studies varies from study to study based on the interests of the researcher, and these interests affect not only the questions asked but also the sample design. Almost all SR studies, however, have included basic demographic information about the respondent's sex, age, race and family SES. Then, depending on the researcher's interests, a series of questions concerning various other independent variables are asked. For example, Short and Nye (1957) were interested in whether respondents who came from broken homes were more likely to report delinquent activities. Hirschi (1969), who was interested in testing a social control theory, included questions on interest in school and achievement motivation. In the NYS (Elliott et al., 1983) measures of the family structure, work status of the respondent, whether the respondent is in or out of school, perceptions of neighborhood crime and environmental problems, and religious attendance are included. Hindelang et al. (1981) include indices measuring respondents' autonomy, meanness, respect for parents, respect for friends, respect for police, achievement motivation, knowledge, and so on. The types of delinquency that respondents have been asked about in SR studies have ranged from the trivial (defied your parents' authority to their face) to serious (used a club, knife, or gun to get something from someone). Again, there is no single set of offense questions that is used in all studies, although the seven questions employed by Short and Nye (Table 4.1) often appear (albeit, with some modifications) in the sets of questions used. There has been a tendency in more recent studies (e.g., Hindelang et al., 1981; Elliott et al., 1983) to include questions that cover more serious crimes. When this is done, a problem similar to that encountered in the NCSs occurs; that is, for rare events a large sample is necessary to provide reliable measures of rates. As respondents report far fewer incidents in which they beat someone up so badly that they required hospitalization than incidents in which they defied their parents, rates for these more serious incidents are more difficult to measure reliably. Table 4.2 presents the crime questions that were used in the NYS (Elliott et al., 1983). The crimes range from the trivial "lied about age" to "strong armed robbery" and "physical threat for sex." This range of crimes is much wider than that in the original Short and Nye items (Tables 4.1). Additionally, the response categories allow for the recording of more specific frequencies for respondents who engage in a great deal of criminal behavior.

In addition to asking about separate offenses, SR researchers often construct scales or indices of delinquency from the set of questions concerned with delinquent behavior. They realize that reported behavior involving skipping class, lying about age (to get into movies), and having sexual intercourse are different both theoretically and empirically from prostitution and the selling of drugs. Elliott et al. (1983), for example, call the first set status offenses and the second set illegal services. In their report they use seven different scales of offense-specific behavior (felony assault, minor assault, robbery, felony theft, minor theft, damaged property, and drug use); five scales based on offense categories (illegal services, public disorder, status offenses, crimes against persons, and general theft); and five summary scales (school delinquency, home delinquency, index offenses, general delinquency A, and general delinquency B). These scales were constructed using what might be labeled theoretical criteria; that is, the offense-specific scales were constructed on the basis of the type of behavior and the degree of seriousness. Hindelang et al. (1981) constructed five separate scales using cluster analysis to help refine scales that were formed using "theoretical criteria." Some of these (e.g., their drug index and their family and school index) are similar to those used by Elliott et al. (1983).

Self-report studies often present results based on scales as well as individual offenses. An advantage of scales (in addition to summarizing data) is that the results of analyses are based on more delinquency items and, thus, tend to be more reliable. A disadvantage is that scales may conceal important differences between the items that make up the scale (e.g., females may have scores similar to males' on a delinquency index, but have lower scores on the serious offenses contained in such an index).

TABLE 4.2
The National Youth Survey Delinquency Items

This section deals with your own behavior. I'd like to remind you that all your answers are confidential. I'll read a series of behaviors to you. Please give me your best estimate of the *exact number* of times you've done each thing during the last year from Christmas a year ago to the Christmas just past. (Record a single number, not a range, and "0" if respondent never engaged in a behavior. For any behavior that the respondent has engaged in 10 or more times in the last year, also record response in the second column.)

	Once a Month	Once Every 2-3 Weeks	Once a Week	2-3 Times a Week	Once a Day	2-3 Times a Day
How many times in the *last year* have you:						
Purposely damaged or destroyed property belonging to your *parents* or other *family members?*	1	2	3	4	5	6
Purposely damaged or destroyed property belonging to a *school?*	1	2	3	4	5	6

These and similar questions were used to ascertain the prevalence and incidence of the following offenses in 1980:

1. Damaged family property
2. Damaged school property
3. Damaged other property
4. Stole motor vehicle
5. Stole something GT $50
6. Bought stolen goods
7. Thrown objects
8. Run away
9. Lied about age
10. Carried hidden weapon
11. Stole something LT $5
12. Aggravated assault
13. Prostitution
14. Sexual intercourse
15. Gang fights
16. Sold marijuana
17. Cheated on school test
18. Hitchhiked
19. Stolen from family
20. Hit teacher
21. Hit parent
22. Hit student
23. Disorderly conduct
24. Sold hard drugs
25. Joyriding
26. Liquor for minor
27. Sexual assault
28. Strongarmed students
29. Strongarmed teachers
30. Strongarmed others
31. Evaded payment
32. Public drunkenness
33. Stole something $5-50
34. Stole at school
35. Broke into bldg/vehicle
36. Panhandled
37. Skipped classes
38. Didn't return change
39. Suspension
40. Obscene calls
41. Used checks illegally
42. Fraud
43. Pressured for sex
44. Physical threat for sex
45. Credit card fraud
46. Arson

The most recent SR studies carefully differentiate the prevalence of reported behavior from the incidence of reported behavior. Prevalence refers to the number of persons reporting one or more behaviors of a given type within a specified reference period whereas incidence refers to the number of behaviors that occur in a reference period. Thus, "the prevalence rate is typically expressed as the proportion of persons in the population who have reported some involvement in a particular offense or set of offenses" (Elliott et al., 1983: 18). Incidence rates are often expressed as the "average number of offenses per person, or as the number of offenses per some population base (e.g., 100, 1000 or 100,000 persons)" (Elliott et al., 1983: 19). Results are then published in terms of both prevalence and incidence. Incidence rates are more comparable to *UCR* data on crimes known to police as they are based on the number of incidents known to the police.

Table 4.3 presents both prevalence and incidence rates for a series of scales from the 1980 NYS. The prevalence rate indicates the percentage of respondents reporting involvement in one or more offenses in a particular category. Thus, 62% of the respondents claimed to have been involved in a status offense during 1980, whereas only 2% claim to have been involved in a robbery. The incidence rates are reported as the average number of incidents per respondent. The average number of status offenses per respondent is 18.07, whereas the average number of robberies is only .10. It is clear that involvement in delinquency of some kinds is widespread among youth, whereas involvement in more serious crimes is relatively rare. The rates in Table 4.3, however, are much higher than either *UCR* or NCS data would suggest (see Chapter 5 for a more detailed discussion).

Scale scores are based on the answers to a number of separate questions about delinquency. In the NYS incidence scale scores for a given individual are based on the sum of the admitted number of acts for all crimes on that scale. The prevalence score for an individual is based on whether he or she admits to one or more acts that are included on a given scale. Relationships may differ depending on whether an individual item or a scale is used. Elliott and Huizinga (1983: 153), for example, point out that "there are substantial differences (by race) in the reported frequency of sexual assault, aggravated assault, and simple assault on parents and teachers." When these scales are combined into a general assault scale, these racial differences disappear because the relationship of race to simple assault is the opposite of its relationship to the other

TABLE 4.3
Prevalence and Incidence Rates from the 1980 NYS

Offense-Specific Scales	Prevalence	Incidence
Felony assault	9	.29
Minor assault	21	1.20
Robbery	2	.10
Felony theft	9	.44
Minor theft	15	1.09
Damaged property	15	.64
Hard drug use	17	5.79
Offense-Category Scales		
Illegal services	11	4.50
Public disorder	48	10.33
Status offense	62	18.07
Crimes against persons	24	1.60
General theft	18	1.53
Summary Scales		
School delinquency	56	8.89
Home delinquency	14	.70
Index offenses	12	.62
Fraud	5	.65

SOURCE: Elliott et al. (1983) adapted from Tables 4.29 and 4.40. Prevalance represents the percentage admitting to one or more acts in that category during the past year. The incidence rates represents the average number of reported delinquent acts in that category during the past year. The age range of respondence was 15 to 21.

two types of assault and because simple assault is a more frequent form of behavior.

Many SR studies have included data concerning not only self-reported criminal activities but also data concerning officially recorded criminal behavior (see Gould, 1969; Hirschi, 1969; Elliott and Voss, 1974; Hindelang et al., 1981). The results of these studies will be reviewed in a later section of this chapter.

WHAT SR DATA EXCLUDE

The SR method allows the researcher to ask offenders and nonoffenders a variety of questions concerning their behavior, perceptions, and attitudes. For this and other reasons the method has great potential for the study of the etiology of criminal behavior. SR research, however, has some practical limitations that are inherent in the method itself, as well as some gaps that have not been filled by previous studies.

Information concerning the geographic distribution of crime based on SR studies is even more limited than that obtained from the NCSs. The most extensive study to date is the NYS that is based on approximately 1,500 respondents. This sample size is sufficient to generate reliable prevalence and incidence rates for the nation as a whole on most of the delinquent behaviors included in the interviews, but it is not large enough to allow detailed breakdowns by geographic area (e.g., rates for states or cities). The only breakdowns by geographic area that are reported for the NYS are those for urban, suburban, and rural areas. Even the massive samples involved in the NCS (60,000 households) are not sufficient to provide reliable estimates for any but the largest geographic areas. When estimating nationwide crime rates for counties, cities, and so on, the *UCRs* are the only statistically reliable (not necessarily valid) source of data. It would, of course, be possible to estimate rates for a city by the SR method, but it would require the funding of a study for that city. There are no plans for a series of such studies comparable to the city surveys conducted by the NCS in the early 1970s.

The focus of SR studies has been on the offender. This is, to some extent, inherent in the method that involves questions about the criminal/delinquent behaviors of the respondents. SR studies have not been used to examine the characteristics of the victims of crime. They could, of course, do so by asking respondents to identify characteristics such as the sex, age, and race of their victims. Thus, this method provides us almost no information about the victims of crime.

The method has most often been used with juvenile, white, in-school populations and, therefore, its coverage has been limited. Past research has not focused on the location or timing of offenses. Little research has been done on the relationship between the offender and victim. These and many other topics could be, but have not been, covered using the SR method. Further research may well address some of these issues.

PROBLEMS WITH SR DATA

SR data are gathered using survey methods and, thus, share many of the strengths and weaknesses of these methods.

A major problem involves the response rates typical of SR studies. In the methodological study by Hindelang et al. (1981) only about 50% of the original sample agreed to participate. Importantly, the rates of participation differed for different groups of potential respondents. For example, only 48.5% of the black females who were official court cases in the original sample were located, and only 55.7% of those located agreed to participate. For black males who were official court cases, 70.4% of the original sample were located and 66.8% of those located agreed to participate (Hindelang et al., 1981: Table 22). Commenting on this problem in a review of the Seattle methods study, Elliott (1982: 528) states that "losses appeared to be selective, with females, blacks and court-identified delinquents being underrepresented in the participating sample. These losses are so great that participating subjects can no longer be considered a probability sample of Seattle youth aged fifteen through eighteen." In an attempt to compensate for this problem, Hindelang et al. (1981) used a system of weights so that the sex, race, SES of census tract, and official deliquency of their sample were representative of the Seattle youth population. This procedure, however, does not guarantee representativeness on other variables.

Even in the best financed surveys there are substantial problems with response rates. For the NYS (Elliott et al., 1983), a sample of 2,360 eligible youths was selected. Of these, 73% agreed to participate in 1976. By 1980 the sample size was down to 1,494, or 63% of the original sample. Although Elliott et al. (1983) argue that the loss of subjects from the initial through the final interview was not highly selective on the basis of race, class, sex, or place of residence (urban/suburban/rural), there is no such guarantee for the subjects in the original sample who refused to cooperate or for self-selection on other relevant variables. To the extent that respondents differ from nonrespondents, the sample is not representative.

Until Short and Nye's (1957) study, many social researchers believed that the SR method would not work because people would not admit to negative behaviors. After all, the social desirability effect had been well documented in survey research; for example, people overestimate their contributions to charities and their frequency of voting in elections. It would seem unlikely, therefore, that they would admit to criminal or delinquent behaviors. The results were surprising to many social scientists; respondents admit to a great deal of delinquent behavior (see Table 4.3). This does not mean that respondents do not underreport (or even overreport) delinquent behavior, but at least a large number of respondents are not too embarrassed to admit to delinquent behavior. Many studies now have been conducted to evaluate both the reliability and validity of respondents' reported behavior.

The reliability of SR data is well established. Hindelang et al. review several studies that have used test-retest, alternate forms, and internal consistency measures of reliability (e.g., Cronbach's alpha); they conclude that "with the exception of test-retest results over a number of years), self-report items appear to behave with notable consistency. If self-report measurement is flawed, it is not here, but in the area of validity" (1981: 84). The question of validity is, of course, more difficult to answer.

One approach used to address the validity question has been to examine the concurrent validity of the SR measures by assuming that those respondents with official recognition as delinquents (e.g., those in a training school or with a court record) should have higher scores on an SR delinquency scale than those without records. This technique has been used since Short and Nye's (1958) original work with SR measures. For example, Short and Nye found (using a Guttman scale) that 86% of the high school boys in their sample had a delinquency score (scale type) of 9 or less, while only 14% of the boys from training schools had scores of 9 or less. Erickson and Empey (1963), in a study of Provo, Utah youth, using a SR survey with 22 items, found that the average number of admitted delinquent acts was related to the official status of the respondent. Those with no official record had an average of 158 acts, one-time offenders averaged 184 acts, repeat offenders on probation 855 acts. Hindelang et al. (1981) also found statistically significant ($p < .001$) differences in offending rates among nondelinquents, police delinquents, and court delinquents on SR measures.

Another technique used to access the validity of SR measures involves the comparison of self-reports of official delinquency (admission of official contact) with official police and court records. Although Short and Nye did not use this validation technique, it was used in the early 1960s by Erickson and Empey (1963). Of 130 respondents who had been to court, every single one mentioned this in their interviews. Hardt and Peterson-Hardt (1977) found no police record for 95% of their respondents reporting no record. Hindelang et al. (1981) found moderate to strong correlations of respondents' self-reported number of times picked up by the police, self-reported number of times referred to the courts by the police, and an index of self-reported official contacts with official measures of these three variables for both males and females. Somewhat lower correlations were found between several self-reported delinquency scales (not self-reported contact) and official measures.

A potential validity problem with SR measures is the possibility of the differential validity of SR measures for blacks and whites. Specifically, the validity of SR measures may be less for blacks than for whites. An indication of this problem appears in some results from Hirschi's (1969) study of Richmond, California youth, in which some 4,000 junior and senior high school students were surveyed. In response to the question, "Have you ever been picked up by the police?" 16% of the white males who said they never had been picked up by the police had police records. Among blacks, 36% of those who said they never had been arrested had police records. Hindelang et al. (1981) found that the correlation between SR measures of delinquency and official measures are typically twice as large for white males (about .60) as for black males (about .30) across a variety of scales (1981: Table 5.8). This effect is consistent across different survey methods. For example, when comparing the percentage of offenses known to the police that were not self-reported, the rate is 9% for white delinquents using questionnaires and 37% for blacks. For the interview method, the rates are 11% for whites and 31% for blacks. Again, the picture that emerges is one of differential validity of self-reports for blacks and whites. At the very least, the agreement between SR and official measures is less for blacks than for whites.

Some further data on this problem are available from the NYS. Here (with a national sample), Elliott et al. (1983) estimate that more than one in five youths with an arrest have concealed their involvement and that underreporting is greater among black than white males. Furthermore, underreporting is more likely to involve serious (index) offenses than nonserious offenses. They suggest, however, that these results might reflect the differential validity of official records (e.g., police might only report the clearly serious crimes of whites but report less serious crimes for blacks) rather than the differential validity of the self-report measures. In spite of some uncertainty concerning the differential validity of SR data, Hindelang et al. (1981) caution against comparisons of delinquency rates for black males with other groups, and Elliott et al. (1983: 37) state that "racial comparisons must be interpreted with caution."

One problem with the tests of validity cited above is that is is difficult to know how strongly official records and self-reported measures of delinquency should correspond. After all, one of the reasons for using the SR method is the claim that official measures are biased; that is, that the real distribution of crimes committed by offenders does not correspond well to that recorded by the police. Not only are they filtered, but the filter is a selective one. Another problem is lack of fit between the acts described on SR schedules and those recorded by the police. The problem is that SR measures are seldom constructed to correspond to the official definitions and procedures used by the police (Hindelang et al., 1981: 88). This problem was not discussed explicitly in some of the early SR studies. The concern is that SR studies measure a number of acts that are too trivial to be recorded by the police. An examination of Table 4.1 reveals a number of behaviors that are unlikely to be viewed as crimes by the authorities: for example, "Ever disobeyed your parents?" or even "Had a fist fight with one other person?" Only chronic incorrigible behavior of this sort is likely to be reported to or acted upon by law enforcement agencies. Many other activities by juveniles (as well as adults) are likely to be handled informally by the police. A major factor in whether a behavior is labeled as a crime is its seriousness. There has been a movement in recent SR research to include items on survey schedules that reflect more serious criminal behavior (compare Tables 4.1 and 4.2).

The seriousness distinction between various types of crimes is important. In the Seattle study the ratio of the percentage of males divided by the percentage of females having ever committed a theft depends on the seriousness of the theft. For whites, the sex ratio is 1.21 for thefts of less than \$2 and 9.60 for thefts of more than \$50. The sex ratios for blacks are in the same direction, but smaller: 1.39 for thefts under \$2 and 2.63 for thefts greater than \$50. A similar trend was found by Hirschi (1969) for the ratio of black to white offenders in Richmond, California. The ratio is .90 for thefts less than \$2 and 1.75 for thefts greater than \$50, but these findings were not replicated in the Seattle data for blacks and whites. Results from the first wave of the NYS (Elliott and Ageton, 1980) also indicate the importance of examining rates of crime within specific crime categories. They find that for illegal services, public disorder, hard drug use, and status offenses the ratio of black to white offenders is either less than one or close to one (with no statistically significant differences). For predatory crimes against property, however, the ratio is 2.30 ($p < .001$), and for predatory crimes against persons the ratio is 1.65 (albeit, it is not quite statistically significant). They find that such differences appear only when mean frequencies are compared and not when the proportions of youth reporting one or more offenses (prevalence measures) are compared. That is, these differences are due, in large part, to a greater proportion of blacks who commit a large number of delinquencies.

These more refined measures of self-reported delinquency have brought into question the findings of several early SR studies that found little if any difference in rates of delinquency for blacks and whites. There seems to be an emerging view that black males report more frequently the types of behavior that are likely to lead to official police contact and to the recording of that contact. That is, they are more likely to commit more serious crimes and there are larger proportions of black males than white males among the most frequent self-reported offenders (Elliott and Ageton, 1980; Hindelang, et al., 1981).

These new measures also shed some light on a recent controversy: the relation between the socioeconomic status of parents and the criminal behavior of youth. This controversy was initiated nearly 30 years ago by Nye and Short (1957), who found no relation between the socioeconomic status of parents and self-reported delinquent behavior, and the controversy has flourished in the criminological literature (see Braithwaite, 1981; Elliott and Voss, 1974; Hindelang et al., 1979; Hirschi et al., 1982; Kleck, 1982; McDonald, 1969; Reiss and Rhodes, 1961; Tittle et al., 1978; Toby, 1960). Using their more refined measures, Elliott and Ageton (1980) found that lower-class youth admit to four times as many attacks on persons as middle-class youth, and that the proportion of lower-class to middle-class offenders increases as the frequency of offenses increases. They conclude, "not only are the relative *proportions* of blacks and lower-class youth higher at the high end of the frequency continuum, but also, within the high category, blacks and lower-class youth report substantially higher *frequencies* than do white and middle-class youth" (1980: 104). A more recent article by Elliott and Huizinga (1983) reports similar results based on all five waves of the NYS. The issue, however, is not closed. A lively debate on the relation of class and criminal activity continues in the literature (Braithwaite, 1981; Elliott and Ageton, 1981; Tittle and Villemez, 1977; Tittle et al., 1978).

Two other issues raised in SR studies are the effects of using a questionnaire versus an interview and the effects of making surveys anonymous or nonanonymous. Given the potentially sensitive nature of the information requested in SR studies of delinquent behavior, one might argue that the best method is an anonymous questionnaire. Here, respondents have some added assurance of the confidentiality of their responses and do not have to admit "bad" behavior to even a single interviewer. Others, however, have argued reasonably that the interview situation allows the researcher to probe the respondent's replies to questions. Thus, when a theft is admitted, it is easier to determine the circumstances surrounding the theft, the value of the object taken, and so on (Erickson and Empey, 1963). Nonanonymous surveys may be necessary for panel research designs or for comparing respondents' answers with official records. The effects of these differences of administration were examined in the Seattle methods research (Hindelang et al., 1981: 133). Their general conclusion is that "no method consistently out performs the other methods and no method is consistently inferior to the other methods in terms of the validity coefficients produced." They make similar statements with regard to the reliability of measures and the relation of SR measures of delinquency to other theoretically relevant variables (e.g., need for achievement, respect for teachers, and parental supervision). Although the relationships are not identical, they often are similar and there is no clear pattern of superiority for one method of administration over another.

It deserves mentioning again that there is no single SR technique. SR studies have been carried out using different methods of administration: anonymous versus nonanonymous, questionnaire versus interview (at times with lie detectors). They have been based on different samples, from high school students in three small Washington communities (Short and Nye, 1958) to the national panel sample of the NYS. Different sets of questions have been used and these sets have been broken down into subscales in various ways. Investigators have included their own sets of independent variables that they relate to self-reported delinquency. In addition, they have scored delinquent behavior in a number of different ways: using prevalence or incidence rates and asking questions that allow specific estimates of the frequency of delinquent activity rather than "never," "once or twice," and "three times or more" (Elliott and Ageton, 1980).

This diversity in approach could be regarded as a weakness of the SR method. After all, how are researchers to establish a cumulative body of research results from studies based on shifting methods with noncomparable samples, questions, and so on. This diversity, however, also may be viewed as a strength. It has allowed researchers to continue to experiment with and refine the technique in a large number of small-scale studies. The NCSs paid a price by not having a 20- to 30-year period of small-scale surveys conducted by a large number of researchers who were not tied to making sure later measures allowed replication of earlier findings. It seems fair to say not only that SR studies have the potential to improve, but that they have been improved substantially over the past decade.

SOME REASONABLE USES OF SR DATA

SR studies provide yet another picture of the volume and distribution of crime and delinquency. This picture is not based on the law enforcement (official) perspective or on the perspective of victims of crime, but on data from offenders. The picture that emerges is one of a large amount of undetected crime. The coverage of self-reported delinquencies also taps crimes that are so trivial that they are not reported in police records or covered in victim surveys, but may, nonetheless, be of interest to students of deviance (e.g., sexual relationships, drinking behaviors, and cheating on exams). More serious types of crimes also can be tapped by SR methods. The NYS, for example, taps all of the Part I *UCR* offenses except for homicide and over 60% of the Part II offenses. The NYS provides incidence and prevalence rates broken down by age, sex, race, social class, and place of residence (urban, suburban, and rural) for the nation as a whole with which the reports of police and victims can be compared. This picture adds to our understanding of the production of official crime rates as well as the distribution of unreported offenses, as the low proportion of offenses that result in arrest may not be representative of all offenses and those people detected may not be representative of all people committing the offenses (Elliott et al., 1983).

The major use of SR studies has been to examine the development of delinquent behavior. This method, after all, is one that focuses on the offender. It is possible to ask offenders about delinquent behavior, their background, attitudes, and even to assess their personality characteristics. This provides a rich source of data from which to formulate and/ or test theories concerning the etiology of delinquent behavior. The NYS, for example, has two explicit purposes: One is to provide a picture of the volume and distribution of the delinquent behavior of American youth and the other is to test an integrated theory of delinquency. SR studies, however, can be much less ambitious than the NYS in terms of coverage and, thus, can be used relatively inexpensively to test other theories concerning the development of delinquent behavior.

SR data can be used as a corrective to, and as a supplement for, data collected by official sources and victimization studies. It can be placed side-by-side with the results from these other two methods to compare, not only the distribution and frequency of criminal behavior, but also other findings generated using these other sources of data. In the next chapter some of these comparisons are made and some interesting convergences and divergences in research employing these three different methods of tapping criminal behavior are examined.

SUMMARY

SR studies first gained popularity in criminological research in the 1950s. They rapidly became the dominant source of data for investigating the etiology of crime. SRs are based on asking samples of respondents whether they have been involved in one or more of a series of criminal/delinquent acts. Respondents also are queried about their backgrounds, attitudes, statuses, and other factors that might be related to delinquent/criminal behaviors.

There is no standard SR methodology; the sets of SR offense questions researchers use have varied from trivial delinquencies to serious crimes (Part I offenses). Background and attitude questions have varied in accordance with the aims of the research. Interviews and questionnaires, anonymous and nonanonymous responses, and convenience and national probability samples have been employed. Several trends are evident, however, that should create a more standardized method. Researchers currently are asking about a wider range of crimes (from trivial to serious) and are allowing a wider range of responses in terms of frequency of offending behavior. Clear distinctions are being drawn between prevalence and incidents rates and the problems of interpreting scales are now widely recognized.

DISCUSSION QUESTIONS

1. What are the advantages of *not* having a standard SR methodology (e.g., the same sets of questions and the same format for questioning)?
2. What are the disadvantages of not having a standard SR methodology?
3. What are some of the reasons that SR studies report higher rates of crime than either the *UCRs* or NCSs?
4. In comparison to the *UCRs* and NCSs, how is the SR method especially well suited to investigate the etiology of crime on the individual level?

5

CRIME RATES BASED ON *UCR*, NCS, AND SR DATA:
Convergence and Divergence

In the last three chapters three major techniques of gathering crime data have been reviewed. Their coverage in terms of the information that each method includes or excludes has been examined and a number of problems with data gathered and reported in the three sources have been discussed. In this chapter the results derived from these three sources of crime statistics are compared in terms of the absolute amount of crime recorded by each method, the demographic characteristics of offenders, the ecological distribution of crimes, and the trends in crime rates.

These comparisons are important as they indicate the extent to which the results of studies of criminal behavior depend on the method by which data are gathered. They also bear on the issue of the validity of the data gathered using these three techniques, as they may be used to assess the convergent validity of the data. The rationale for using covergence as an indicator of validity is that if the data collected using different methods are measuring the same underlying phenomenon, they ought to yield similar results. Thus, if the patterns generated by *UCR*, NCS, and SR data are similar, this is consistent with the idea that all three methods are measuring the same underlying phenomenon. If the data patterns are not consistent, this raises questions about the validity of one or more of the measures. After all, if both the *UCR* and SR methods are measuring the same phenomenon (e.g., the relative rates of female and male assaults) they ought to agree with each other concerning estimates of the sex ratio for those involved in aggravated assault. If they do agree, this supports the validity of both measures; and if they don't, it brings into question their validity as measures of the ratio of male offenders to female offenders.

Throughout this chapter, it is important to note that measures may be valid for one purpose and not for another. The *UCRs* may not be valid as measures of the absolute amount of aggravated assault, but may be relatively valid indicators of the sex ratio of aggravated assault offenders. Furthermore, the measurement of some crime rates (e.g., vehicle theft) may show more convergence than others (such as aggravated assault).[1] Before comparing data generated by these three techniques, however, some problems with comparing data from these sources are discussed.

PROBLEMS OF COMPARABILITY

A major problem with comparing *UCR*, NCS, and SR data involves the equivalence of the nominal definitions of crimes employed by each method. Fortunately, at lease some reports have used similar nominal definitions. The NCS data on criminal incidents and the SR study of Elliott et al. (1983) (i.e., the National Youth Survey) intentionally used *UCR* definitions of crimes in the construction of their survey instruments. Exceptions to this involve homicide, about which questions are not asked in either the NCS or NYS studies, and larceny for which the NCS covers only household and personal larcenies and excludes larcenies from commercial establishments. Although the nominal definitions may be considered similar enough to compare some crimes measured by each of the methods, their operational definitions (e.g., how data on these variables are gathered and crime rates measured) are, of course, different. It is convergence in the face of different operational definitions that we are attempting to assess.

A second issue involves the comparability of the populations covered by the studies, as convergence should not be expected unless results are based on the same populations. Such comparisons are reasonably well justified at least for national estimates of crime rates from the *UCR*, NCS, and the NYS studies as both the NCS and the NYS are based on probability samples of the United States as a whole. For the *UCRs*, the reporting agencies represent over 97% of all people in the nation. There are, however, some problems in this area of comparability. For example, the NCSs only ask about victimizations involving individuals aged 12 and over, whereas the *UCRs* are based on crimes known to the police regardless of the age of the victim. The NYS, on the other hand, covers juveniles from ages 11 to 18 in the first wave of the survey and from ages 15 to 21 in the fifth wave (the panel aged during the course of the research). Differences in the ages covered probably does little to affect the overall estimates of the number of crimes based on the *UCRs* and the

NCSs, as few children are victims of the Part I crimes reported in the NCSs and, if involved, few of these crimes are likely to be reported to the police (Nelson, 1978). For the NYS data, comparisons are limited to data from the *UCRs* and NCSs that involve a similar age range.

When comparing city-level NCS and *UCR* data, a further problem involves the populations on which city-level *UCR* and NCS data are based. The *UCRs* record crimes that occur within the city, whereas the NCSs record crimes that have occurred to residents of the city, whether they occurred within the city or not, and does not include victims of crimes that occurred in the city who do not live within the city. Thus, comparisons involving city-level data from these two sources are comparisons of results from somewhat different populations. This particular difference, however, should not greatly influence reported rates. A study conducted by Garofalo (1977) found that over 93% of all personal victimizations reported in the NCS city surveys occurred in the resident's home cities. Thus, one might expect the city *UCR* rates to be somewhat inflated as "the number of persons within a city is ordinarily larger than the number of residents" (Nelson, 1978: 5) and the *UCR* rates are based on the number of known crimes divided by the number of residents and not by the number of people within the city. This problem may affect the estimated rates of crime in cities differentially, as cities may have different proportions of commuters and visitors.

A major difference between the three data sources has to do with how incidents "get into" the records. Both the NCS and SR methods ask respondents about crimes (albeit, the NCSs about victimizations and SRs about offenses). The *UCR*, however, is based on crimes that become known to police and are, therefore, further removed (in terms of filters) from the incidents than are the NCS or SR data. For a crime to become known to the police, someone must report it or the police must discover it themselves. As the police tend to be reactive rather than proactive (Black, 1973)—that is, they react to reports of crime more often than they discover crimes themselves—we can expect the volume of crimes known to the police to be smaller than the volume reported by respondents in either the NCSs or SRs. This should affect the validity of the *UCRs* as a measure of the actual amount of crime, but it may not affect its use in measuring the demographic characteristics of offenders (e.g., the sex ratio of offenders or proportion of black offenders) and in ecological studies of crime rates.

There are many other differences that could affect comparisons. For example, crimes known to the police are subjected to more or less rigorous unfounding procedures whereas NCS and self-reported crimes are not. Some NCS and SR studies are unbounded and, thus, may result in incidents being telescoped forward or backward into or out of the reference period (see Chapter 3). Series victimizations, especially in the NCS and some SR studies, can cause serious undercounting of the number of criminal incidents. This problem was discussed for the NCSs in Chapter 3 and is a problem with many SR studies that have response categories for delinquent behavior such as "never," "once or twice," and "three times or more" (Elliott and Ageton, 1980).

Given these problems of comparison, one might well ask, "Why attempt comparisons?" The answer is that if these sources of data do not give similar answers to questions about the rates of crime, the characteristics of offenders, the ecological correlates of crimes, or trends in crime rates, the results of much criminological research may be to a large extent method dependent. One theory may be supported by SR data and refuted by *UCR* data, while another contradictory theory is supported by NCS data and refuted by SR data. Thus, it is important to examine the degree to which these multiple methods of collecting data yield similar or divergent results.

CONVERGENCE OF ABSOLUTE RATES

As the above discussion indicates, caution must be exercised when making comparisons among these three sources of data. For example, Table 5.1 presents data from the NCS for 1976 and the *UCR* for 1976 on the number and rate (per 1000) of criminal incidents in the United States. Data from the NYS are not used in this particular comparison because they are based solely on the responses of youth about their criminal activity. The year 1976 was chosen because it was the last year in which the NCS gathered data on commercial robberies and burglaries as well as personal robberies and household burglaries. Both types of robberies and burglaries are included in the *UCR* figures. The data in Table 5.1 from the NCS for personal crimes are based on incidents (not victimizations) so as to be more comparable to the *UCR* data. Data on larcenies has not been included in the table because the NCS does not collect data on commercial larcenies (e.g., shoplifting). Although vehicle theft has been included in the table, this comparison between *UCR* and NCS data is somewhat suspect as the NCS does not include the theft of commercially owned vehicles and these account for almost 10% of the motor

TABLE 5.1
National Crime Rate Estimates for Rape, Aggravated Assault,
Robbery, Burglary, and Motor Vehicle Theft Based on
Uniform Crime Reports and National Crime Surveys (1976)

	NCS		UCR		
	Number	Rate	Number	Rate	NCS/UCR
Rape	145,193	(.68)	56,730	(.26)	2.56
Aggravated assault	1,694,941	(7.90)	490,850	(2.29)	3.45
Robbery	1,390,155	(6.48)	420,210	(1.96)	3.31
Burglary	7,774,061	(36.22)	3,089,800	(14.39)	2.52
Motor vehicle theft	1,234,644	(5.75)	957,600	(4.46)	1.29

SOURCE: NCS data are from Table 3.2 in *The Sourcebook of Criminal Justice Statistics–1982* Flanagan and McLeod, 1983). Business and personal robberies have been added together as have business and household burglary to facilitate comparisons with *UCR* data. The *UCR* data are from Table 3.53 in *The Sourcebook of Criminal Justice Statistics–1982* Flanagan and McLeod, 1983).

vehicles in the United States. Thus, the *UCR* and NCS estimates of crime rates in Table 5.1 should be generally, although not perfectly, comparable.

The differences between the absolute level of crimes estimated from NCS and *UCR* data is striking. On the low end the ratio of NCS to *UCR* crimes is 1.29 for motor vehicle theft and on the high end 3.45 for aggravated assault. For all crimes, except vehicle theft, over two times as many crimes are recorded in the NCS than appear in the *UCR* data. It is clear that NCS and *UCR* crime rates do not converge in terms of the absolute amount of crime except in the case of vehicle theft, for which the two rates are about 30% apart. As was pointed out in Chapters 2 and 3, neither source reflects the true rate of crimes and it is not likely that any method of collecting data will pinpoint the absolute amount of crimes such as rape and aggravated assault.

The problems involved in comparing *UCR* and NCS absolute crime rates to SR absolute crime rates are formidable. Before attempting to draw some limited comparisons, some problems that have hampered past comparisons should be reviewed. A major factor involves the nature of the samples used in most SR studies. They have tended to be small and, as noted in Chapter 4, often have been based on juveniles. As *UCR* data on the number of crimes known to the police and much NCS data are not broken down by the age of offenders, it is difficult to compare these data.

A second factor that has limited comparisons of NCS, *UCR*, and SR data is what Hindelang et al. (1979) refer to as the "domain problem." They point out that SR surveys generally ask questions about relatively nonserious offenses (e.g., skipped school without a legitimate excuse or had sexual relations with a person of the opposite sex). One study found that of the final seven items on the Short and Nye SR scale (see Table 4.1), no item ranked higher than 125th out of 140 items that were rated for seriousness (Rossi et al., 1974).

Recently, some attempts have been made to collect data on more serious crimes. The most comprehensive SR study is the NYS (Elliott et al., 1983). This study is national in scope and contains questions about a wide range of crimes. Further refinements (e.g., care in avoiding a single act being counted as more than a single criminal incident and allowing a wider range of responses in terms of the frequency of individual acts, see Elliott and Ageton, 1980) make this SR study more comparable to *UCR* and NCS data in terms of absolute crime rates.

Even using these data, however, our comparisons will be crude. For example, if results from the 1976 NYS are used so that they can be compared to results in Table 5.1 that are based on the *UCR* and the NCS for the same year, the NYS has data on only 11-17 year olds. This is certainly not comparable to data from the NCS and *UCR* that are based on the total population. Still, SR data are available from a national sample and for some crimes covered in the *UCRs* and NCSs. Bearing in mind that the rates in Table 5.1 are estimated rates for the total population for the *UCR* and for those 12 and over for the NCS, I will tentatively compare them with 1976 rates based on 11-17 year olds. This comparisons is biased in terms of finding higher crime rates for the NYS sample. The incident rate for aggravated assaults in the NYS is 170 (per 1000) and for robbery is 290 (per 1000). This compares with rates of 7.90 and 6.48 based on the NCS and 2.29 and 1.96 for the *UCR*.[2] A large part of this discrepancy is due to differences in the age groups, but not all of it can be so easily explained. For example, in 1976 11-17-year-olds comprised 13.38% of the U.S. population, whereas those under 11 contributed 16.93% of the population.[3] Thus, even if it were assumed that no assaults or robberies were committed by those over 17 years of age, the almost 22 fold (170/7.90) difference between NYS estimated assault rate and NCS estimated assault rate and the 45 fold (290/6.48) difference in NYS and NCS robbery rates could not be explained solely on the basis of differences in the age groups on which they are based. Even when the crimes compared are similar and serious, the SR method estimates a much larger absolute rate of crime than do either the NCS or *UCR*.

Determining the absolute crime rate is a chimera. Whether a given behavior is a crime or not depends in part on the perspective that one brings to the situation. Imagine, for example, the situation of an aggravated assault. The "offender" may feel that no crime has been committed because the victim "pushed first." The "victim" may (or may not) think that the offender's use of increased force was "ok" given the situation and, therefore, was not a crime. The police officer investigating the incident may feel that the settlement of the pushing match is better handled informally or that this "criminal incident" is a matter for arrest. The legal system represented by lawyers will dispute whether the act was a crime (if the incident gets that far) and a judge ultimately may define the act as a criminal act or not. The judge's decision may be appealed and even if the offender loses, he or she still may not define the act as a crime. It is, thus, not surprising that the volume of crimes estimated to have occurred during a given year differs depending on whether victims or offenders are asked or whether estimates are based on official police records.

CONVERGENCE OF RELATIVE RATES
ACROSS GEOGRAPHIC AREAS

Even though *UCR*, NCS, and SR studies yield divergent results with respect to the absolute amount of crime, they might well provide similar results when used as measures of the relative amount of crime across geographic areas (e.g., SMSAs or states). That is, it may be that victims report to interviewers far more crimes than come to the attention of the police, that police record only some of the crimes that come to their attention, and so on, but that these biases are fairly constant across geographic locations. If this were the case, even though aggravated assault is reported to interviewers at a rate three to four times greater than appears in the *UCRs*, the relative rate of crimes for, say, Los Angeles and Chicago still could be ascertained using either method. If this were the case, it would support the use of both NCS and *UCR* crime data in what might be labeled ecological studies of crime (e.g., Blau and Blau, 1982; Decker et al., 1982; Harries, 1974, 1980; Loftin and Hill, 1974; Schuessler, 1962; Shaw and McKay, 1969). These studies do not simply describe which areas have the highest crime rates, but investigate the relation of crime rates to, for instance, population density, age structure, income inequality, racial composition, and region. Note that crime rate data may converge (and/or be valid) for some purposes (comparing relative rates of crime) even if they do not converge for others (estimating the absolute rate of crime).

Although it would be possible for a simple constant bias to exist across police jurisdictions such that NCS rates would be a given percentage higher than *UCR* rates, it is not likely given the evidence that *UCR* crime rates are dependent on a series of factors that vary from one police jurisdiction to another. Many of these factors were reviewed in the Chapter 2: for example, organizational pressures to keep crime rates down (Seidman and Couzens, 1974; Selke and Pepinsky, 1982), a crackdown on particular crimes in a given community (Defleur, 1975), differences in the processing of crimes (McCleary et al., 1982), differences in local laws (Beattie, 1960; U.S. Department of Justice, 1981a), the degree of professionalism in law enforcement agencies (Beattie, 1960; Skogan, 1976; Wilson, 1978), the styles of police enforcement (Wilson, 1978), and the workload of police officers (Maxfield et al., 1980).

UCR crime rates are not the only crime rates that may vary from one geographic unit to the next due to factors other than the actual rate of crime. For example, the reporting rates in the NCS vary from city to city. That is, the percentage of crimes that citizens say occurred and that they say they reported to the police varies from city to city. At one extreme, 34% of the victims of rape said they reported this victimization to the police in Houston whereas 75% of the victims of rape in Newark said they reported this crime to the police. For the crime of commercial burglary, however, the range of reporting was smaller, from 68% to 84%. Table 5.2 shows the range of reporting that was found in the 26 cities surveyed in 1974-1976.

Further problems with the comparability of NCS data across jurisdictions were discussed in Chapter 3: for example, the large sampling and interviewer variance (Bailey et al., 1978) associated with city-level estimates of crime rates. These differences are large enough that the differences among cities "may be obscured by sampling and nonsampling variances" (Bailey et al., 1978: 23). Other problems—for example, that the NCSs ask about crimes occurring to those 12 and above and the *UCRs* are focused on crimes at any age, that the *UCR* data are based on crimes occurring in the city and NCS data are based on crimes occurring to residents of the city—have been mentioned earlier in this chapter.

No matter what the reasons for expecting *UCR* and NCS rates to have different patterns across geographic areas, it is important to

TABLE 5.2

Lowest, Highest, and Median Percentages of Crimes Reported to Police, NCS City Surveys, 1974-1975

	Percentage of Crimes Reported to the NCS Interviewer and Said to Have Been Reported to the Police		
	Lowest	*Highest*	*Median*
Personal and household crimes			
Simple assault	28	45	32
Robbery without a weapon	33	61	43
Aggravated assault	41	62	49
Rape	34	75	53
Burglary	46	58	54
Robbery with a weapon	50	72	60
Motor vehicle theft	63	80	73
Commercial victimizations			
Robbery without a weapon	48	94	65
Burglary	68	84	77
Robbery with a weapon	79	100	93

SOURCE: Nelson (1978: Table 1).

determine the extent of this lack of convergence. Are such factors important enough to obscure the relations between the structural characteristics of cities (e.g., population density, poverty, inequality) and crime rates? Are they, and other factors, important enough to change our conclusions about these relations depending on whether *UCR* or NCS data are used? If so, one might argue that the conclusions reached by various investigators are highly dependent on the source of the data used to estimate crime rates.

A number of studies have investigated the convergence of NCS based crime rates and *UCR* based crime rates for the 26 cities included in the NCS city surveys (Booth et al., 1977; Cohen and Lichbach, 1982; Decker, 1977; Nelson, 1978, 1979; O'Brien et al., 1980). Below, I present results from Nelson (1978: Table 3). Table 5.3 contains the correlations (Pearson's product moment) between the NCS and *UCR* derived crime rates for these 26 cities for each of seven crimes. These correlations have been computed for both all NCS incidents and for only those that victims said they reported to the police. The positive correlation ($r = .91$) between NCS and *UCR* motor vehicle theft rates (based on all incidents) can be interpreted as indicating that those cities with a relatively high motor vehicle theft rate according to NCS data tend to have a relatively high rate according to the *UCR* data. There is surprisingly strong convergence for the rates of motor vehicle theft (r = .91) and robbery with a weapon (r = .81). There is less convergence for burglary (r = .69) and robbery without a weapon (r = .56), and essentially no agreement for simple assault and rape. There is divergence for aggravated assault (i.e., for this crime there is a tendency for those cities with relatively high rates according to the NCS to have relatively low rates according to the *UCR*). Clearly, the degree of convergence depends on the type of crime under investigation. It is perhaps not surprising that the crime showing the greatest absolute agreement between NCS and *UCR* rates (see Table 5.1) also shows the greatest convergence across geographic areas. The relatively strong convergence for robbery and burglary is more surprising. The results for the three crimes showing the least convergence persisted when Nelson (1978) recalculated the aggravated assault rate to include only persons who had suffered injury and included series victimization for aggravated assault, simple assault, and rape for the NCS data. It should be noted, however, that two crimes that are not included in the NCS surveys—homicide and bank robbery—probably are the most consistently measured across jurisdictions.

An additional question remains: What are the effects of this lack of convergence on the conclusions researchers reach when using either

TABLE 5.3
Percentage of Variance Explained and Zero-Order Correlations
Between the UCR and the NCS Crime Rates

Crime	Variance Explained and Zero-Order Correlations			
	All NCS Victims		NCS Victims Who Said They Reported the Victimization to the Police	
	%	r =	%	r =
Motor vehicle theft	82	(.91)	85	(.92)
Robbery with a weapon	65	(.81)	72	(.85)
Burglary	47	(.69)	53	(.73)
Robbery without a weapon	31	(.56)	48	(.69)
Simple assault	0	(.05)	4	(.20)
Rape	0	(.04)	0	(.07)
Aggravated assault	13	(−.36)	7	(−.26)

SOURCE: Nelson (1978, Table E).
NOTE: *UCR* and NCS rates are based on the population at risk. That is, NCS rates are based on the city's residential population whereas *UCR* rates are based on an estimate of the number of persons who used each city on a daily basis (see Nelson, 1978, for further details).

UCR or NCS based crime rates. The answer again depends on the type of crime involved. A number of researchers have addressed this topic (e.g., Booth et al., 1977; Nelson, 1979; O'Brien et al., 1980). Here, the results of a recent study by O'Brien (1983) are discussed. O'Brien attempted a partial replication of a study by Blau and Blau (1982) using not only *UCR* data, but also NCS city-level crime rates. The results indicate a lack of convergence in the findings based on these two different measures for the crimes of assault and rape. Table 5.4 presents the correlations between the crime rates for aggravated assault, robbery, and rape based on both *UCR* and NCS data and the percentage of the population who are black and the percentage below the Social Security Administration's poverty line. Only in the case of robbery rates are the correlations based on *UCR* and NCS estimates in the same direction. For aggravated assault, there is a strong positive correlation with poverty and the percentage of blacks for the *UCR* aggravated assault measure and a strong negative correlation for the NCS measure. Conflicting results also occur for the *UCR* and NCS measures of rape. Thus, the degree of convergence between the results based on *UCR* and NCS crime rates depends on the type of crime under consideration. For at least some crimes, the findings from studies investigating the structural correlates of crime rates appear to be method dependent.

Zedlewski (1983) draws a similar conclusion with regard to deterrence findings. Using 1977 *UCR* and NCS data on 137 SMSAs, he finds that "UCR-based measures of apprehension risk and criminal activity uncover no relationship between apprehension risk and crime rates while comparable NCS-based measures find a strong deterrent effect" (Zedlewski, 1983: 262).

TABLE 5.4
Zero-Order Correlations of *UCR* and NCS Crime Rates
With Percentage Black and Poverty

	Percentage Black		*Poverty*	
	NCS	*UCR*	*NCS*	*UCR*
Assault	−.45	.47	−.42	.50
Robbery	.32	.64	.22	.49
Rape	−.26	.43	−.13	.14

NOTE: The log to the base 10 of all crime rates was used to make the results comparable to those in Blau and Blau (1982). However, the results are substantially the same whether or not this transformation is made.

CONVERGENCE OF DEMOGRAPHIC
CHARACTERISTICS OF OFFENDERS

The results of the third comparison of crime rate data from different sources (*UCR*, NCS, and NYS) are rather encouraging. Here, I compare measures from each of these sources to see how well they converge with respect to the "demographic characteristics of offenders." For example, how closely do data from these sources agree with regard to the percentage of male and female offenders or of black and white offenders? Do data from these sources converge with regard to the relative rates of offending by social class or by age? A series of comparisons of NCS victimization and *UCR* arrest data with respect to the sex, race, and age of offenders have been conducted by Hindelang (1978, 1979, 1981). In his 1978 and 1979 articles, Hindelang examined the convergence of NCS and *UCR* data in terms of the relative amount of crime committed by males and females and by blacks and whites. Data from the *UCRs* are based on arrests, as it is at this point that information about the sex and race of offenders is recorded. Data from the NCSs are based on victim's recall of the sex and race of offenders. The data in Table 5.5 are based on Hindelang's 1978 and 1979 articles and include the four crimes from the NCS for which offenders and victims must come into contact and, thus, allow for the identification of the offender's sex and race.

The convergence of these two sets of data with respect to the sex of offenders is quite impressive. Only for robbery and aggravated assault are there discrepancies. In both cases males make up a larger percentage of the *UCR* offenders than the NCS offenders, but even here the discrepancy is not large. Using either *UCR* or NCS data, researchers would conclude that for these serious crimes males predominate in terms of offending behavior. Hindelang (1979) conducted some more problematic comparisons between *UCR* and NCS rates for burglary, motor vehicle theft, and larceny. These are less comparable because victims usually do not see the offenders in these crimes and, in the case of larceny, *UCR* and NCS rates are not comparable for other reasons (see Chapter 3). In any case, the convergence is almost perfect for burglary (NCS males make up 95% of the offenders and *UCR* males 95%) and motor vehicle theft (NCS males make up 94% of the offenders and *UCR* males 93%). There is substantial divergence in the case of larceny; males comprise only 69% of the *UCR* offenders, whereas they comprise 82% of the NCS offenders. The *UCR* and NCS definitions of larceny differ,

TABLE 5.5
Comparison of Arrestees in *UCR* and Estimated Number
of Offenders in the NCS Data by Race and by Sex

		% White	% Black	% Other	% Male	% Female
Rape	NCS	60	39	1	99	1
		(52)	(47)	(1)		
	UCR	49	48	3	99	1
Robbery	NCS	34	62	4	93	7
		(30)	(65)	(4)		
	UCR	35	62	3	96	4
Aggravated Assault	NCS	66	30	4	87	13
		(70)	(26)	(4)		
	UCR	56	41	2	92	8
Simple Assault	NCS	66	29	5	86	14
		(69)	(26)	(5)		
	UCR	61	37	2	86	14

SOURCES: Hindelang (1978: Tables 1 and 2), Hindelang (1979; Table 1). The data for race are based on *UCR* and NCS estimates for 1974 and for sex on 1976 estimates. Figures in parentheses are based on those NCS offenses that victims claim to have reported to the police.

however, with the NCS not including shoplifting, a crime in which women participate in large numbers (Cohen and Stark, 1974; Hindelang, 1974).

There is somewhat less convergence between NCS and *UCR* data with regard to the race of offenders. Except for the crime of robbery, the *UCR* estimates the percentages of black offenders to be greater than estimates based on NCS data. In the case of aggravated assault this discrepancy is 11%, for rape it is 9%, and for simple assault it is 8% (see Table 5.5). Hindelang notes that part of these discrepancies may be due to the fact that crimes involving black offenders are not reported to the police as often as those involving whites. There is some evidence for this contention based on NCS interviews (Hindelang, 1978: 103). When considering only those crimes that victims said they reported to the police (see figures in parentheses in Table 5.5) the discrepancy between *UCR* and NCS estimates of the percentages of black and white rape offenders is substantially diminished. Although the convergence is not perfect, using either the NCS or *UCR* data one would conclude that blacks comprise a larger proportion of offenders than their representation in the general population would warrant.

A final comparison of the agreement of *UCR* and NCS estimates of the demographic characteristics of offenders involves the joint distribution of the age, sex, and race of offenders for the same crimes that appear in Table 5.5 (Hindelang, 1981). Again, some discrepancies are found, but the trends in NCS and *UCR* data are similar. For example, both data sets indicate that black males between the ages of 12 and 20 offend relatively more often than do white males, who offend relatively more often than do black females, who offend more often than do white females in the same age category. The rates for all groups of offenders are less for those 21 and over than for those 12 to 20 (for those of the same sex and race). Hindelang (1981: 472) concludes, "the findings presented here in the form of incidence rates of offending parallel the findings in most sources of arrest data." There is a fair degree of convergence with regard to the demographic characteristics of offenders based on these two sources of data.

During the early years of SR studies it generally was thought that the results of SR and official measures of crimes were inconsistent with regard to relative rates of offending by sex, race, and social class. There is, however, a growing consensus that, at least in the case of race (percentage of black and percentage of white offenders) and sex (percentage of male and percentage of female offenders), official and SR measures converge if steps are taken to make the data comparable. The most important steps are insuring that the crimes compared are of the same type and seriousness (Hindelang et al., 1979) and that the response sets employed in SR measures allow for differentiation of offenders with a high frequency of offense from those with other levels (Elliott and Ageton, 1980). The effects of crime seriousness on the convergence of crime rate measures for the *UCR*, NCS, and SR studies are examined first.

UCR Part I crimes and the crime data collected by the NCS are based on serious crimes. Much of the "crime" data collected in SR studies has concerned relatively minor offenses (e.g., skipped school without a legitimate excuse, defied parents to their face, and so on). The sex ratios (ratios of male to female offenders) for such crimes are near one. Additionally, such crimes often have been combined into scales of delinquent activity and the sex ratio has, of course, been near one. When this ratio was compared to that for *UCR* data (such as the data in Table

5.5), the *UCR* ratio of male to female offenders was much larger than 1.0. Thus, in the early days of SR studies there was a tendency to conclude that most of the differences between male and female rates of offending in official records were based on some sort of bias due to factors such as reporting, recording, and selective enforcement. There was, however, in these early studies, a tendency for the sex ratio to increase as the crimes in question became more serious. In a review of the literature, Hindelang et al. (1979) computed the median sex ratio for crimes of varying degrees of seriousness that were reported in a number of studies. They found that the median sex ratio for runaways was 1.00, drinking and truancy, 1.28, but for more serious crimes such as taking a car (3.37), gangfight (3.28), beatup/assault (3.61), theft over $50 (3.68), and strong armed robbery (2.87), the sex ratio was much higher. The sex ratio for these serious crimes was closer to those based on *UCR* and NCS estimates (Hindelang et al., 1979: Table 1).

There also is some convergence of SR with *UCR* and NCS crime rate estimates with respect to the ratio of black to white offenders, although this evidence is somewhat less solid given the relatively small number of blacks that appear in most SR studies. There is, however, a trend in many SR studies that shows increasing ratios of blacks to whites with the increasing seriousness of crimes (Hindelang et al., 1979). For example, Berger and Simon (1974) found a slightly greater involvement of whites than blacks in "normal deviance" (e.g., skipping school, cheating on exams, drinking); their theft scale (e.g., property damage, theft of little things, keeping or using stolen goods) showed no differences; their violence scale (e.g., used weapon, been in gang fight, strong armed robbery) produced consistently higher crime rate ratios of blacks to whites.

Further evidence comes from the NYS, in which response categories were designed to capture a larger range of the frequency with which crimes are committed (see Elliott and Ageton, 1980). Using this scale and a national sample, they found statistically significant differences in the mean levels of offending by blacks for predatory crimes against property (a ratio of 2.30) and for overall self-reported delinquency (a ratio of 1.69) and nearly significant differences for predatory crimes against persons (a ratio of 1.65). One reason for this finding is that blacks predominate at the high end of the frequency scale (e.g., 9.8% of blacks reported 200 or more delinquent offenses whereas only 4.1% of the whites did). A similar finding was reported by Hindelang (1973). He found that the sex ratio increased from 1.72 for those involved in "one or more recent acts" to 6.00 for those involved in "five or more recent acts."

Although there are no *UCR* data on the social class of offenders, there are a number of studies that have shown that lower-class individuals are somewhat more likely to be recorded as offenders in police records. Examination of a number of SR studies shows a weak but consistent negative relation between social class and rates of criminal offense across a wide range of studies (Hindelang et al., 1979: Table 5). Similar, rather weak effects are seen in data from the NYS (Elliott and Ageton, 1980). For example, they found the mean frequency for total self-reported delinquency to be 60.42 for lower-class respondents, 50.63 for working-class respondents, and 50.96 for middle-class respondents. For predatory crimes against persons, the means are 12.02 for lower-, 8.04 for working-, and 3.32 for middle-class respondents. Finally, for predatory crimes against property, the means are 13.50 for lower-, 9.40 for working-, and 7.25 for middle-class respondents.

Overall, there is a fairly high degree of convergence for the three data sources with regard to the demographic characteristics of offenders. Although the agreement is not perfect, data from all three sources indicate that offense rates are higher among blacks than whites and males than females. *UCR* sex ratios for Part I offenses based on arrest data agree almost perfectly with NCS sex ratios based on victim identification of offenders. The ratio of black offenders to whites based on *UCR* arrest data and NCS victim identifications is not as close, with the proportion of blacks being somewhat greater in the *UCR* data for some crimes. In any case, using either source of data, blacks are overrepresented among offenders in comparison to the proportion of the population that they comprise. Finally, both males and blacks are overrepresented among offenders in SR studies when serious crimes are considered and response categories allow for a large number of offenses. Just how much criminal justice system bias there is remains an open question, but the greater offense rates of males and blacks is indicated by each of these three methods.

CONVERGENCE OF CRIME TRENDS

It is possible to compare *UCR* and NCS based crime trends for the years since 1973. Table 5.6 shows the trends from 1973 to 1981 for rape, motor vehicle theft, and aggravated assault rates as estimated by both *UCR* and NCS data. Only in the case of rape are the trends somewhat similar. For rape, the product moment correlation is .46 (p > .05). For motor vehicle theft, the correlation is only .04 (p > .05), and for aggravated assault, it is -.68 (p < .05: two-tailed). Overall, these results do not indicate a high degree of convergence of crime trends based on these two data sources. It should be noted, however, that these are very short series (9 years) with a relatively small degree of variation in crime rates from year to year. These facts limit the utility of these comparisons and make conclusions drawn from these comparisons tentative.

A different comparison of crime trends has been made by Messner (1984). He investigated the average annual percentage change in the rates of crime as reflected in various crime indices. He found that "regardless of the weighting system, the average annual increase in the NCS indexes is less than 1%. The indexes based on UCR data reveal much more appreciable increases in crime between 1973 and 1981— from 3.5% to 5.0%" (Messner, 1984: 44).

It also is possible to compare seasonal trends in NCS and *UCR* crime rates. When this is done for motor vehicle theft and aggravated assault, the trends seem to be somewhat similar. Both data sets indicate that motor vehicle theft rates are lower during the first half (than in second half) of the year and that aggravated assault rates are highest during the warmer months and lower during the winter months.[4]

In Chapter 6 the implications for researchers and policy-makers of the comparisons made in this chapter and of the discussions of each

TABLE 5.6
Rates (per 100,000) for Rape, Aggravated Assault, and
Motor Vehicle Theft from 1973 to 1981

	1973	1974	1975	1976	1977	1978	1979	1980	1981
Rape									
NCS	177	182	165	144	157	167	184	179	183
UCR	24	26	26	26	29	31	34	36	36
Aggravated assault									
NCS	1007	1039	961	986	998	969	992	921	964
UCR	200	216	227	229	242	256	279	291	281
Motor vehicle theft									
NCS	818	813	845	718	745	775	781	751	772
UCR	443	462	469	446	448	455	498	495	469

SOURCE: *UCR* data are from the FBI (1982: Table 2, p. 39) and NCS data are from the U.S. Department of Justice (1983). *UCR* rates are based on number of inhabitants; NCS rape rates are based on the number of women 12 and over and motor vehicle theft and aggravated assault rates are based on the population age 12 and over.

method of gathering crime data from the previous chapters are examined. For example, how can data from each of the methods be appropriately used? What additional data should be collected and/or reported from each source? What uses of these data are contraindicated by these analyses?

SUMMARY

Crime rate data from the *UCRs*, NCSs, and SR studies converge for some types of comparisons and not for others and for some crimes and not for others. The data do not converge in terms of the absolute rates of crime, except for motor vehicle theft for which *UCR* and NCS rates are somewhat similar. For serious crimes, all three data sources indicate that in relation to their proportion in the population, males offend substantially more than do females, blacks more than whites, and youth more than the middle-aged or elderly. This convergence is encouraging given early indications that SR and official records diverged substantially with regard to the demographic characteristics of offenders. There remains, however, some evidence of an overrepresentation of blacks in official records. Examinations of the ecological distribution of crimes indicate that *UCR* and NCS crime rates (for 26 cities) are in substantial agreement with respect to relative rates of crime across large central cities for motor vehicle theft and robbery with a weapon; moderate agreement for burglary and robbery without a weapon; and essentially no agreement for simple assault, rape, and aggravated assault. It is too early to judge whether data from these sources will converge with regard to trends in crime rates over time, but preliminary results are not encouraging.

DISCUSSION QUESTIONS

1. Aggravated assault and rape data show the least convergence across the different types of comparisons made in this chapter. Why do you think this lack of convergence exists.?
2. Motor vehicle theft shows the most convergence across the different types of comparisons made in this chapter. Why do you think this convergence exists?

3. Although we have no comparative data on arson rates from the *UCRs*, NCSs, and SRs, do you think that the absolute number of arson incidents is likely to be accurately reported? Is the relative rate of arson across geographic areas likely to be accurately reported?

4. How is it possible for the absolute rate of crimes as measured by the *UCRs* and NCSs to diverge so greatly for robbery and burglary (see Table 5.1) and yet to show a moderate to high degree of convergence in terms of the relative rates across cities (see Table 5.3)?

NOTES

1. It is important to distinguish between convergence and validity. Convergence is an indicator of validity. If measures converge, their validity is supported. If they fail to converge, one or more of the measures are not valid as measures of a single phenomenon. Convergence is relatively simple to establish, but validity is elusive. Before making even tentative statements about the validity of a measure, an investigator should consider several types of evidence besides convergence: for example, studies that indicate whether data collection is biased, an examination of the content of the measure, or the theoretical definition of the phenomenon.

2. These estimates are from Elliott et al. (1983). The estimate for robbery is from Table 4.32 and the estimate for aggravated assault is from 4.16. The measure of aggravated assault does not include gang fights (300/1000) or sexual assaults (40/1000), which Elliott et al. include in their felony assault scale (Table 4.32).

3. These population estimates are from the U.S. Bureau of the Census (1977: Table 1).

4. These results are based on an examination of a U.S. Department of Justice (1980) publication entitled *Crime and Seasonality*. This publication does not include data on rape (presumably because of the limited number of cases reported by respondents each month). The seasonal trends for *UCR* data are found in the annual publication, *Crime in the United States*.

6

CONCLUSIONS:
Social Science and
Social Policy Implications

The importance of using multiple measures of social phenomena is widely recognized in the social sciences. In Chapter 5 multiple measures were used as an aid in assessing the accuracy of crime data from the *UCRs*, the NCSs, and SR studies. In many instances, the use of one data source or another resulted in highly divergent findings (e.g., when comparing the absolute rates of crime or the relation between aggravated assault rates based on NCS city surveys and those based on *UCR* assault rates for the same 26 central cities). In other instances, data converged to a high degree, such as data on the relative offense rates of males and females and data on seasonal trends in crime rates. Such convergence does not prove that the different methods of gathering statistics on crime are tapping the same underlying phenomenon; they do, however, add to our confidence in the conclusions that we draw from these data sources. Below, some implications of the analyses in the previous chapters are examined for the light they shed on both the social scientific use of crime data and their use as guides for social policy decisions. Then the issue of upgrading criminal statistics briefly is addressed.

ASSESSING THE ABSOLUTE RATE OF CRIME

It is virtually impossible to assess the absolute rate of most crimes (e.g., rape, aggravated assault, larceny, and vandalism). This is reflected in a lack of convergence for comparisons involving crime rates from the *UCRs*, NCSs, and NYSs and is consistent with many of the studies reported in Chapters 2-4. For example, *UCR* crime rates depend on the direct detection of crimes by police or the reporting of crimes by citizens as well as other processes involved in the official recording of crimes. Survey-generated rates (NCSs and SRs) depend on such factors as respondent recall, willingness to report, meaningful bounding points for interviews, and so on. These problems are severe enough that our confidence in estimates of the absolute rate of crimes generated from any of these sources is not high. There are, however, some exceptions; for example, the homicide rate as measured by the *UCRs* is probably accurate as are statistics on commercial robberies (especially bank robberies). There is also a fair degree of agreement between motor vehicle theft estimates based on *UCR* and NCS data.

The situation for most other crimes is much more ambiguous. In these cases, attempting to measure the absolute rate of crime is difficult. For example, how should we decide whether an assault has occurred. Police will be interested in legal definitions, evidence, whether complainants or witnesses will press charges, as well as other considerations, whereas the victim and offender may disagree about whether the assault was justifiable, worth reporting, or whether one or both of them share some responsibility. Thus, one or both might admit that a crime occurred and possibly neither would report it. Further complications arise because this crime often involves friends or relatives. For crimes such as assault and rape, it may never be possible to obtain accurate estimates of the rate of offense.

For both scientific and policy purposes, it is important to recognize that the absolute rates of different crimes are not all equally well measured. Again, there is reason to believe that the number of homicides in the United States (as estimated by the *UCRs*) is not as greatly underestimated as the number of aggravated assaults. Furthermore, the proportion of aggravated assaults that involves family members is almost certainly higher than that reflected in either the *UCRs* or the NCSs, as police are more reticent to become involved in family affairs and citizens are less likely to report incidents involving family members either to the police or to interviewers. Many of the crime rates based on crimes known to the police are underestimated and most experts would agree that NCS estimates are closer to actual crime rates. There are some, however, who think that the NCSs record a large number of relatively trivial crimes (Levine, 1976, 1978; Chambliss, 1984).

COMPARISONS ACROSS GEOGRAPHIC AREAS

The warning in *Crime in the United States* (FBI, 1982) that the *UCR* crime rates should not be compared across jurisdictions is ignored by many researchers. The evidence supporting this warning is overwhelming and comes from a number of different types of studies, for example, comparisons of laws across jurisdictions (Beattie, 1960; U.S. Department of Justice, 1981a); implausible differences in rates across geographic regions (Beattie, 1960; Inciardi, 1978); historical studies following crime crackdowns (Defleur, 1975) or other changes in police policy (Seidman and Couzens, 1974; Selke and Pepinsky, 1982); the effects of organizational changes within departments (McCleary et al., 1982) and analyses of styles of policing (Wilson, 1978).

The comparisons in Chapter 5 of *UCR* and NCS crime rates across cities, however, suggest that some examination of rates across geographic areas may be legitimate. When these rates are compared across 26 cities, there is a high degree of convergence for motor vehicle theft ($r = .91$) and robbery with a weapon ($r = .81$) and a moderate degree of convergence for burglary ($r = .69$) and robbery without a weapon ($r = .56$). There was almost no convergence for simple assault, rape, and aggravated assault, all crimes of personal violence. There is evidence to suggest that these crimes are poorly measured by both the *UCRs* (Chapter 2) and NCSs (Chapter 3). One personal crime of violence that is probably well measured for comparative purposes is homicide.

The implication for both social scientists and policy-makers is that comparisons of crime rates across jurisdictions for personal crimes of violence (with the exception of homicide) are problematic when using *UCR* data. Comparisons using homicide rates and motor vehicle data are relatively well supported and those for burglary and robbery may be more valid than previously had been suspected. These comparisons are important, for they may suggest relationships between income inequality, racial segregation, household crowding, and crime rates for cities. Such comparisons, however, face many interpretive problems (see Roncek, 1975), especially those involving the use of aggregate-level data.

The NCSs might seem to provide a better source of data for comparing crime rates across jurisdictions as they are based on standardized data collection instruments, use standardized interviewing and sampling procedures, and are coded and analyzed in a standardized manner. This should ameliorate several of the problems involved in making comparisons of crime rates across a number of police jurisdictions.

There are at present, however, a number of problems with using these data for either scientific or policy purposes when making comparisons across geographic areas. Some of these problems could be overcome by putting more resources into the NCSs. This is true of the large sampling errors associated with regional and statewide data from the NCS national surveys and is even a problem with the NCS city surveys that were based on 10,000 households per city. The problem is that very large sized samples are needed to provide reliable enough estimates of rare events (such as rape or assault) to allow for comparisons across cities or other geographic areas (see Figure 3.3). This problem is compounded by interviewer variance (Bailey et al., 1978). A second potential problem is that there may be systematic differences in the reporting behavior of respondents from one geographic area to another. Certainly, there is evidence that respondents differ in the proportion of reported victimizations that they claim to have reported to the police (see Table 5.2). It is possible that they also vary in terms of the proportion of victimizations that they report to NCS interviewers.

Potentially, the most difficult obstacle to using NCS data for cross-jurisdictional comparisons is a response effect that has been noted by a number of researchers (Penick and Owens, 1976; Skogan, 1981; Sparks, 1981). Specifically, in the NCSs more highly educated respondents (both black and white) report a substantially higher rate of victimization by assault (see Chapter 3). Skogan (1981) suggests that this may be due to differential respondent productivity, in that more educated respondents are more cooperative and at ease in the interview situation. It also might be due to differences in definitions of a criminal assault that are related to education. In either case, neither Skogan (1981: 12) nor Sparks (1981: 34) believe that these rates reflect true differences in victimization rates across educational levels. This response bias could play havoc with comparisons of crime rates across different areas. The problem is that differences in average education across, for example, central cities is related to differences in median income, percentage black, population density, and so on. If cities with above average education have above average assault rates because of this response bias, then cities with low population density, high median income, and a low percentage of blacks will tend to have higher rates of assault. This single response bias could invalidate cross-jurisdictional comparisons using NCS data.

Before the NCSs are instituted again to gather data on cities or other smaller (or larger) geographic units, the problem of possible response biases (e.g., respondents in one city reporting a smaller percentage of crimes due to level of education, race, or some other variable) must be thoroughly investigated and solved. Until that time, there is little to offer either policy-makers or scientific researchers in the way of a data set that allows comparisons of personal crime rates across jurisdictions. It is important to note, however, that comparisons involving homicide and motor vehicle theft, and possibly robbery and burglary as well, may be legitimate.

There have been only two national studies of self-reported delinquency/ crime (Gold, 1966; Elliott et al., 1983). The sample sizes for these studies preclude any but the crudest of regional comparisons. For example, Elliott et al. (1983) provide comparisons of rates for urban, suburban, and rural areas. Other studies have compared rates for a sample of midwestern versus western high school students, but such comparisons are of limited generalizability, especially in comparison with the large number of areas covered by the *UCRs*. Although SR studies comparable to the NCS city studies could be developed, this is not likely to occur.

DEMOGRAPHIC CHARACTERISTICS OF OFFENDERS

The comparisons in Chapter 5 of *UCR* arrest rates, NCS victim identifications of offenders, and SR studies involving the demographic characteristics of offenders were encouraging (although there are indications of a "criminal justice system bias" against blacks in the *UCR* data). The results with regard to the ratio of male to female, black to white, and young to old offenders were in agreement, at least in terms of which groups are more likely to commit Part I offenses. The degree of agreement between *UCR* arrest data and NCS data based on victim identification of the sex, race, and, in a crude way, the age of offenders is somewhat surprising given the evidence of a potential response bias based on education in the NCSs. In the case of race, we might well have expected such a bias to create a large gap between the ratio of black to white offenders for *UCR* and NCS data. That is, if blacks underreport assaults (as they tend to have less education) and blacks are more likely to be assaulted by blacks than whites, then the ratio of black to white assault rates based on NCS data should be relatively low in comparison to that found using *UCR* data. On the other hand, most studies (see Chapter 2) that report an effect, find that blacks are somewhat more likely to be arrested than whites for similar types of crimes. This should lead to a higher ratio of blacks to whites in arrest figures than there actually is in "true offense figures." The two sets of figures, those based on NCS and *UCR* estimates, however, are fairly similar (see Table 5.5).

In any case, the data from either source indicates that blacks and males are substantially overrepresented (with respect to their proportion of the population) in the offender category. Similar results have been produced in SR studies that focus on serious crimes and allow for the recording of large numbers of reported offenses (see Hindelang et al., 1981; and Elliott and Huizinga, 1983). Thus, it appears that in this area—the demographic characteristics of offenders—data tentatively may be used for testing scientific theories and making generalizations as well as for policy purposes. This does not mean that the data should be used blindly, as there are still questions concerning, for example, interpersonal crimes. But the results of three rather different methods of gathering these data converge and add to our confidence in the results. There is some limited data that indicate a possible convergence of official and SR data with respect to the social class of offenders. These analyses are based on the records of police departments and data collected in SR studies (Elliott and Huizinga, 1983; but see Hindelang et al., 1981).

CRIME TRENDS

In my comparisons of *UCR* and NCS crime trends for the period 1973 to 1981, I found a low degree of convergence. For two of the crimes examined (rape and motor vehicle theft) the relationship was positive but not statistically significant. The lack of statistical significance is not surprising, given the short series, but the Pearson correlation for motor vehicle theft is only .04 and that for rape .46. Furthermore, the correlation between the two series for aggravated assault is strongly negative ($r = -.68$). These results are not encouraging. There are no appropriate SR series with which to compare *UCR* and NCS series because of differences in the age range of the populations covered and the short length of existing SR series.

Furthermore, there is some evidence that crime trends are affected by changes in administrative policies and funding (e.g., Defleur, 1975; McCleary et al., 1982; Seidman and Couzens, 1974). Whether such policies somehow balance out on a national level is an open question. Given the existence of national-level crime programs and a national media, such an assumption may not be tenable. Again, of course, some crimes such as homicide and commercial robberies may well provide valid time series. With regard to seasonal trends, I found that *UCR* and NCS estimated crime rates tended to converge for both motor vehicle theft and aggravated assault (the only two crimes examined).

As with data from any source, individual analysts are ultimately responsible for deciding whether a particular set of data should be used in a given situation. For example, extreme fluctuations in the rate of burglary as estimated by the *UCRs* may not be plausibly explained as an artifact, but may more reasonably be attributed to a depressed economy or increased opportunity due to new light-weight, hard to protect consumer goods. The analyst, however, is responsible for this decision and should be aware of the limitations of the data.

SOME SUGGESTIONS FOR
UPGRADING CRIMINAL STATISTICS

There currently is underway comprehensive studies evaluating and recommending changes in both the *UCRs* and NCSs. Recommendations for changing the NCS are being developed under the direction of Albert Biderman at the Bureau of Social Research in Washington, D.C., and for the *UCRs* by Abt Associates. Below, I will examine some relatively inexpensive ways in which criminal statistics could be upgraded.

Uniform Crime Reports

The *UCRs* could collect data that would identify the sex, race, and age of the offender at the stage of crimes known to the police, using the simple expedient of reporting the complainant's report of this information. This procedure is used in the NCSs when victims are asked to identify the sex, race, and (crudely) age of offenders for crimes such as rape, robbery, and aggravated assault that involve contact between the victim and offender. This type of data gathering effort would be consistent with Sellin's (1931: 346) dictum that "the value of a crime for index purposes decreases as the distance from the crime itself in terms of procedure increases." This procedure would collect data on the basic demographic characteristics of offenders before the filtering processes that lead to arrest have come into play. Uniform Crime Reporting also could include data on the victims (complainants). Again, data on race, sex, and age could be obtained easily and, quite possible, data on other characteristics such as occupation and employment status, and the relationship of victims to offenders. These data would be collected using mechanisms that already are in place and information that already is collected in most police reports. It would require that this information be reported to the Uniform Crime Reporting program.

These data then could be analyzed by examining which groups of victims are at higher risk and, more specifically, what is their rate of victimization. Victim and offender characteristics could be cross-classified to ascertain the extent to which assault involves same sex or same race individuals. With less confidence, the proportion of assaults involving strangers, relatives, and offenders known to the victim could be estimated (and the estimates compared to those obtained from the NCSs). Clearly, these and other analyses would be of interest to both policy-makers and social researchers. Other suggestions that grow out of the analysis in Chapter 2 are the need for more detailed breakdowns of crimes. These suggestions would not require major changes in data gathering procedures: for example, breakdowns of the race, sex, and age of offenders (arrestees) for at least Part I crimes at the level of cities, counties, SMSAs, and states. Currently, this information is only published for Part I crimes for the entire population. The *UCRs* provide detailed breakdowns on homicide victims and offenders (from arrest data) and the same sort of data could be provided for other crimes (e.g., relationships of victim to offender and breakdowns by race, by sex, by age of offenders).

A final suggestion is that the *UCRs* emphasize the problems involved in examining a single crime rate index. Even the examination of the violent crime and property crime indexes can be misleading (see Decker et al., 1982: chap. 4). Therefore, policy-makers and social researchers are strongly encouraged to examine the rates for individual crimes rather than index rates.

National Crime Surveys

The NCSs already collect many of the types of data that I suggested could be collected by the Uniform Crime Reporting program. There is, however, additional information that the NCSs could collect that would greatly increase their utility for policy-makers and social researchers. First, they could collect data on what the National Academy of Science report (Penick and Owen, 1976) called "independent variables" and Sparks (1981) has labeled "contextual" information. For example, the National Academy of Science report suggests collecting data on the ecological vulnerability (e.g., median income of the area, type of land use in an area, whether residential, mixed, or commercial, and the crime rate for an area), status vulnerability (e.g., sex, age, social class), role vulnerability (e.g., husband-wife, parent-child, taxi driver), opportunity (e.g., security guard, bars on window, item identification sticker on door). The relationships of victimization rates to these sorts of variables have obvious policy implications.

A number of suggestions can be made concerning the presentation of NCS data. The first involves the "timeliness" of the publication of NCS results. NCS publications of yearly findings take almost twice as long as those for the *UCR* (which appear in September of the year following the one to which they pertain). Another has to do with the manner in which victimization rates are reported. Skogan (1978) points out that the calculation of victimization rates per auto or for single women makes more sense in many situations that the calculation of rates based on the total population, as these rates tell people their chances of victimization. Similar suggestions could be made for the crime rates reported in the *UCRs* if victim information were collected.

A major effort should be made to establish the accuracy of crimes against persons (rape and assaults) as measured by the NCSs. These two crimes are the most problematic in terms of record checks and their relationships to *UCR* data. The factors that determine the reporting or nonreporting of these crimes must be carefully studied. This is a call for a new series of methods studies on this crucial aspect of NCS data.

Self-Reports

A national SR survey of youth should occur each year and continual refinements be made in that survey. The data from the NYS have shown that this technique for measuring crime rates is feasible and that many of the findings tend to converge with those from the *UCRs* and NCSs. In addition, it provides data on offenders that simply is not available from either the *UCRs* or the NCSs (e.g., personality and attitude measures, parents' SES, respondents' employment status, and age). Furthermore, this procedure is much less expensive than the NCSs, in large part because of the relatively high frequency with which offenders admit to criminal behavior.

Studies should be undertaken to see how well this technique could be extended to include adults as well as youth and methodological studies are needed to investigate potential reporting biases on the basis of race, social class, and education.

SUMMARY

This review of crime statistics led to a number of suggestions for their use. It is virtually impossible to estimate the absolute rates for certain crimes, such as assaults and rapes, whereas the rates for other crimes, such as homicides and commercial robberies, may be quite accurate. The comparison of crime rates across geographic areas may not be as severely limited as the yearly warning in *Crime in the United States* suggests. Crime rates for homicide, auto theft, and certain types of robbery (i.e., robbery with a weapon, commercial robbery, and bank robbery) may be suitable for making comparisons across geographic areas. There is some evidence that the crimes of burglary and robbery without a weapon may be compared (albeit, somewhat more tentatively) across jurisdictions. The warning in *Crime in the United States*, how-ever, should be taken seriously, indeed, for the crimes of assault and rape. The proportion of males and females involved in crime seems to be fairly accurately reflected in *UCR* statistics, but the proportion of blacks and whites may be somewhat less accurately portrayed (especially for rape and assault). There are a number of factors that potentially could invalidate the use of *UCR*, NCS, or SR data for establishing crime rate trends over time, and there is not yet sufficient data to definitively test the convergence of trends based on these three sources. The limited data available, however, are not encouraging. The last section of this chapter was devoted to practical suggestions for the upgrading of data from these three sources.

DISCUSSION QUESTIONS

1. Data based on assaults and rapes seem to be the least comparable across the three data sources. This is true whether interest focuses on absolute rates, comparisons of rates across jurisdictions, or the demo-graphic characteristics of offenders. Discuss why the measures of these rates rather than, for example, burglary or motor vehicle theft, produce such divergent results?

2. Why might you expect homicide rates to be measured accurately enough for use in most sorts of comparisons?

3. What other suggestion for upgrading criminal statistics would you make? How would these particular suggestions lead to better data for social researchers and policy-makers?

APPENDIX

A. Part I Uniform Crime Reporting Offenses

1. Criminal Homicide: Murder and nonnegligent manslaughter: the willful (nonnegligent) killing of one human being by another. Deaths caused by negligence, attempts to kill, assaults to kill, suicides, accidental deaths, and justifiable homicides are excluded. Justifiable homicides are limited to: the killing of a felon by a law enforcement officer in the line of duty and the killing of a felon by a private citizen. Manslaughter by negligence: the killing of another person through gross negligence. Traffic fatalities are excluded. Although manslaughter by negligence is a Part I crime, it is not included in the crime index.

2. Forcible rape: The carnal knowledge of a female forcibly and against her will. Included are rapes by force and attempts or assaults to rape. Statutory offenses (no force used, victim under age of consent) are excluded.

3. Robbery: The taking or attempting to take anything of value from the care, custody, or control of a person or persons by force or threat of force or violence and/or putting the victim in fear.

4. Aggravated assault: An unlawful attack by one person upon another for the purpose of inflicting severe or aggravated bodily injury. This type of assault usually is accompanied by the use of a weapon or by means likely to produce death or great bodily harm. Simple assaults are excluded.

5. Burglary-breaking or entering: The unlawful entry of a structure to commit a felony or a theft. Attempted forcible entry is included.

6. Larceny-theft (except motor vehicle theft): The unlawful taking, carrying, leading, or riding away of property from the possession or constructive possession of another. Examples are thefts of bicycles or automobile accessories, shoplifting, pocket-picking, or the stealing of any property or article that is not taken by force and violence or by fraud. Attempted larcenies are included. Embezzlement, con games, forgery, worthless checks are excluded.

7. Motor vehicle theft: The theft or attempted theft of a motor vehicle. A motor vehicle is self-propelled and runs on the surface and not on rails. Specifically excluded from this category are motorboats, construction equipment, airplanes, and farming equipment.

8. Arson: Any willful or malicious burning or attempt to burn, with or without intent to defraud, a dwelling house, public building, motor vehicle or aircraft, or personal property of another.

B. Part II Uniform Crime Reporting Offenses.

1. Other assaults (simple): Assaults and attempted assaults in which no weapon was used and which did not result in serious or aggravated injury to the victim.

2. Forgery and counterfeiting: Making, altering, uttering, or possessing, with intent to defraud, anything false that is made to appear true. Attempts are included.

3. Fraud: Fraudulent conversion and obtaining money or property by false pretenses. Included are larceny by bailee and bad checks, except forgeries and counterfeiting.

4. Embezzlement: Misappropriation or misapplication of money or property entrusted to one's care, custody, or control.

5. Stolen property; buying, receiving, possessing: Buying, receiving, and possessing stolen property, including attempts.

6. Vandalism: Willful or malicious destruction, injury, disfigurement, or defacement of any public or private property, real or personal, without consent of the owner or persons having custody or control.

7. Weapons; carrying, possessing: All violations of regulations or statutes controlling the carrying, using, possessing, furnishing, and manufacturing of deadly weapons or silencers. Included are attempts.

8. Prostitution and commercialized vice: Sex offenses of a commercialized nature, such as prostitution, keeping a bawdy house, procuring, or transporting women for immoral purposes. Attempts are included.

9. Sex offenses (except forcible rape, prostitution, and commercialized vice): Statutory rape and offenses against chastity, common decency, morals, and the like. Attempts are included.

10. Drug abuse violations: State and local offenses relating to narcotic drugs, such as unlawful possession, sale, use, growing, and manufacturing of narcotic drugs.

11. Gambling: Promoting, permitting, or engaging in illegal gambling.

12. Offenses against the family and children: Nonsupport, neglect, desertion, or abuse of family and children.

13. Driving under the influence: Driving or operating any vehicle or common carrier while drunk or under the influence of liquor or narcotics.

14. Liquor laws: State or local liquor law violations, except "drunkenness" (offense 15) and "driving under the influence" (offense 13). Federal violations are excluded.

15. Drunkenness: Drunkenness or intoxication. Excluded is "driving under the influence" (offense 13).

16. Disorderly conduct: Breach of the peace.

17. Vagrancy: Vagabondage, begging, loitering.

18. All other offenses: All violations of state or local laws, except offenses 1-17 and traffic offenses.

19. Suspicion: No specific offense; suspect released without formal charges being placed.

20. Curfew and loitering laws: Offenses relating to violations of local curfew or loitering ordinances where such laws exist.

21. Runaways: Limited to juveniles taken into protective custody under provisions of local statutes.

C. National Crime Survey Offenses

PERSONAL CRIMES: Rape, robbery, assault, personal larceny with contact, and personal larceny without contact. Includes both completed and attempted acts.

1. Rape: Carnal knowledge through the use of force or the threat of force, including attempts. Statutory rape (without force) is excluded. Includes both heterosexual and homosexual rape.

2. Robbery with injury: Theft or attempted theft from a person, accompanied by an attack, either with or without a weapon, resulting in injury. An injury is classified as resulting from a serious assault, irrespective of the extent of injury, if a weapon was used in the commission of the crime, or if not, when the extent of the injury was either serious (e.g., broken bones, loss of teeth, internal injuries, loss of consciousness) or undetermined by requiring two or more days of hospitalization. An injury is classified as resulting from a minor assault when the extent of the injury was minor (e.g., bruises, black eyes, cuts, scratches, swelling) or undetermined but requiring less than two days of hospitalization.

3. Robbery without injury: Theft or attempted theft from a person, accompanied by force or the threat of force, either with or without a weapon, but not resulting in injury.

4. Aggravated assault: Attack with a weapon resulting in any injury and attack without a weapon resulting either in serious injury (e.g., broken bones, loss of teeth, internal injuries, loss of consciousness) or in undetermined injury requiring two or more days of hospitalization. Also includes attempted assault with a weapon.

5. Simple assault: Attack without a weapon resulting either in minor injury (e.g., bruises, black eyes, cuts, scratches, swelling) or in undetermined injury requiring less than two days of hospitalization. Also includes attempted assault without a weapon.

6. Personal larceny with contact: Theft of purse, wallet, or cash by stealth directly from the person of the victim, but without force or the threat of force. Also includes attempted purse snatching.

7. Personal larceny without contact: Theft or attempted theft, without direct contact between victim and offender, of property or cash from any place other than the victim's home or its immediate vicinity. In rare cases, the victim sees the offender during the commission of the act.

HOUSEHOLD CRIMES: Burglary, household larceny, or motor vehicle theft. Includes both completed and attempted acts.

8. Burglary: Unlawful or forcible entry of a residence, usually, but not necessarily, attended by theft. Includes attempted forcible entry.

9. Household larceny: Theft or attempted theft of property or cash from a residence or its immediate vicinity. Forcible entry, attempted forcible entry, or unlawful entry is not involved.

10. Motor vehicle theft: Stealing or unauthorized taking of a motor vehicle, including attempts at such acts.

COMMERCIAL CRIMES: Commercial burglary and commercial robbery. These categories were discontinued after 1976.

11. Commercial burglary: The unlawful or forcible entry or attempted forcible entry of a commercial establishment, usually, but not necessarily, attended by a theft.

12. Commercial robbery: The theft or attempted theft of money or property from a commercial establishment, by force or threat of force.

UCR definitions are from *Crime in the United States--1982* (FBI, 1982). The National Crime Survey definitions are from *Crime Victimization in the United States 1973-79 Trends* (U.S. Department of Justice, 1981) and the *Dictionary of Criminal Justice Data Terminology* (U.S. Department of Justice, 1981).

REFERENCES

AKERS, R. L. (1964) "Socio-economic status and delinquent behavior: a retest." Journal of Research in Crime and Delinquency 1: 38-46.

AMIR, M. (1967) "Forcible rape." Federal Probation 31: 51-58.

BAILEY, L., T. F. MOORE, and B. A. BAILAR (1978) "An interview variance study for the eight impact cities of the National Crime Survey cities sample." Journal of the American Statistical Association 73: 23-30.

BEATTIE, R. H. (1960) "Criminal statistics in the United States—1960." Journal of Criminal Law, Criminology, and Police Science 51: 49-65.

BELL, D. (1960) "The myth of crime waves," pp. 137-158 in D. Bell (ed.) The End of Ideology: On the Exhaustion of Political Ideas in the Fifties. New York: Free Press.

BERGER, A. S. and W. SIMON (1974) "Black families and the Moynihan Report: a research evaluation." Social Problems 22: 146-161.

BIDERMAN, A. D., L. A. JOHNSON, J. McINTYRE, and A. W. WEIR (1967) Report on a Pilot Study in the District of Columbia on Victimization and Attitudes Toward Law Enforcement. U.S. President's Commission on Law Enforcement and the Administration of Justice, Field Survey I. Washington, DC: U.S. Government Printing Office.

BLACK, D. J. (1980) The Manners and Customs of the Police. New York: Academic Press.

———(1979) "Common sense in the sociology of law." American Sociological Review 44: 18-27.

———(1976) The Behavior of Law. New York: Academic Press.

———(1973) "The mobilization of law." Journal of Legal Studies 2: 125-149.

———(1970) "The production of crime rates." American Sociological Review 35: 733-748.

———and A. J. REISS, Jr. (1970) "Police control of juveniles." American Sociological Review 35: 63-77.

BLAU, J. R. and P. M. BLAU (1982) "The cost of inequality: metropolitan structure and violent crime." American Sociological Review 47: 114-129.

BLOCK, R. (1974) "Why notify the police: the victim's decision to notify the police of an assault." Criminology 11: 555-569.

———and C. R. BLOCK (1980) "Decisions and data: the transformation of robbery incidents into official robbery statistics." Journal of Criminal Law and Criminology 71: 622-636.

BOOTH, A., D. R. JOHNSON, and H. M. CHOLDIN (1977) "Correlates of city crime rates: victimization surveys versus official statistics." Social Problems 25: 187-197.

BRAITHWAITE, J. (1981) "The myth of social class and criminality reconsidered." American Sociological Review 46: 36-57.

CATLIN, G. and S. MURRAY (1979) Report of Canadian Victimization Survey Methodological Pretests. Ottawa: Statistics Canada.

CHAMBLISS, W. J. (1984) "Crime rates and crime myths," pp. 167-177 in W. J. Chambliss (ed.) Criminal Law in Action. New York: John Wiley.

CLARK, J. P. and L. L. TIFFT (1966) "Polygraph and interview validation of self-reported delinquent behavior." American Sociological Review 31: 516-523.

COHEN, J. and M. LICHBACH (1982) "Alternative measures of crime: a statistical evaluation." Sociological Quarterly 23: 253-266.

COHEN, L. and R. STARK (1974) "Discrimination, labelling and the five-finger discount—an empirical analysis of different shoplifting dispositions." Journal of Research in Crime and Delinquency 11: 25-39.

DECKER, D. L., D. SHICHOR, and R. M. O'BRIEN (1982) Urban Structure and Victimization. Lexington, MA: D. C. Heath.

DECKER, S. H. (1977) "Official crime rates and victim surveys: an empirical comparison." Journal of Criminal Justice 5: 47-54.

DEFLEUR, L. B. (1975) "Biasing influences on drug arrest records: implications for deviance research." American Sociological Review 40: 88-103.

DENTLER, R. A. and L. J. MONROE (1961) "Social correlations of early adolescent theft." American Sociological Review 16: 733-743.

DEUKMEJIAN, G. (1981) Crime and Delinquency in California—1980. Sacramento, CA: Division of Law Enforcement.

DODGE, R. W. (1976) "National Crime Survey: comparison screen questions with their final classification, 1975." Washington, DC: U.S. Bureau of the Census, Crime Statistics Analysis Staff. (mimeo)

———(1970) "Victim recall pretest—Washington, DC." Washington, DC: U.S. Bureau of the Census. (memorandum, June 10)

———and A. G. TURNER (1971) "Methodological foundations for establishing a national survey of victimization." Presented at the annual meetings of the American Statistical Association, Social Statistics Division, Fort Collins, Colorado.

ELLIOTT, D. S. (1982) "Review essay: measuring delinquency." Criminology 20: 527-537.

———and S. S. AGETON (1980) "Reconciling race and class differences in self-reported and official estimates of delinquency." American Sociological Review 45: 95-110.

ELLIOTT, D. S. and D. HUIZINGA (1983) "Social class and delinquent behavior in a national youth panel: 1976-1980." Criminology 21: 149-177.

ELLIOTT, D. S. and H. VOSS (1974) Delinquency and Dropout. Lexington, MA: D. C. Heath.

ELLIOTT, D. S., S. S. AGETON, D. HUIZINGA, B. A. KNOWLES, and R. J. CANTER (1983) The Prevalence and Incidence of Delinquent Behavior: 1976-1980: National Estimates of Delinquent Behavior by Sex, Race, Social Class and Other Selected Variables. Boulder, CO: Behavioral Research Institute.

ENNIS, P. H. (1967) Criminal Victimization in the United States: A Report of a National Survey. President's Commission on Law Enforcement and the Administration of Justice. Field Surveys II. Washington, DC: U.S. Government Printing Office.

ERICKSON, M. and L. T. EMPEY (1963) "Court records, undetected delinquency and decision-making." Journal of Criminal Law, Criminology, and Police Science 54: 456-469.

FARRINGTON, D. P. (1973) "Self-reports of deviant behavior: predictive and stable?" Journal of Crime and Criminology 64: 99-110.

FBI (1983) Crime in the United States—1983. Washington, DC: U.S. Government Printing Office.

———(1982) Crime in the United States—1982. Washington, DC: U.S. Government Printing Office.

———(1980) Uniform Crime Reporting Handbook. Washington, DC: U.S. Government Printing Office.

FLANAGAN, T. J. and M. McLEOD [eds.] (1983) Sourcebook of Criminal Justice Statistics—1982. U.S. Department of Justice, Bureau of Justice Statistics. Washington, DC: U.S. Government Printing Office.

FRIEDRICH, R. J. (1977) "The impact of organizational, individual, and situational factors on police behavior." Ph.D. dissertation, University of Michigan.

GAROFALO, J. (1977) Local Victim Surveys: A Review of the Issues. Law Enforcement Assistance Administration, National Criminal Justice Information and Statistics Service, Analytic Report SVAD2 Washington, DC: U.S. Government Printing Office.

———and M. J. HINDELANG (1977) An Introduction to the National Crime Survey. Washington, DC: Criminal Justice Research Center, U.S. Department of Justice.

GOLD, M. (1970) Delinquent Behavior in an American City. Belmont, CA: Brooks/Cole.

———(1966) "Undetected delinquent behavior." Journal of Research in Crime and Delinquency 3: 37-46.

———and D. J. REIMER (1975) "Changing patterns of delinquent behavior among Americans 13-16 years old: 1967-72." Crime and Delinquency Literature 7: 483-517.

GOTTFREDSON, M. R. and M. J. HINDELANG (1979a) "A study of the behavior of law." American Sociological Review 44: 3-18.

———(1979b) "Theory and research in the sociology of law." American Sociological Review 44: 27-37.

GOULD, L. C. (1969) "Who defines delinquency: a comparison of self-reported and officially reported indices of delinquency for three racial groups." Social Problems 16: 325-336.

HARDT, R. H. and S. PETERSON-HARDT (1977) "On determining the quality of the delinquency self-report method." Journal of Research in Crime and Delinquency 14: 247-261.

HARRIES, K. D. (1980) Crime and Environment. Springfield, IL: Charles C Thomas.

———(1974) The Geography of Crime and Justice. New York: McGraw-Hill.

HINDELANG, M. J. (1981) "Variations in sex-race-age-specific incidence rates of offending." American Sociological Review 46: 461-474.

———(1979) "Sex differences in criminal activity." Social Problems 27: 143-156.

———(1978) "Race and involvement in common law personal crimes." American Sociological Review 43: 93-109.

———(1976) Criminal Victimization in Eight American Cities. Cambridge, MA: Ballinger.

———(1974) "The Uniform Crime Reports revisited." Journal of Criminal Justice 2: 1-17.

———(1973) "Causes of delinquency: a partial replication and extension." Social Problems 20: 471-487.

———T. HIRSCHI, and J. G. WEIS (1981) Measuring Delinquency. Beverly Hills, CA: Sage.

———(1979) "Correlates of delinquency." American Sociological Review 44: 995-1014.

HIRSCHI, T. (1969) Causes of Delinquency. Berkeley: Unversity of California Press.

———M. J. HINDELANG, and J. G. WEIS (1982) "Reply to 'on the use of self-reported data to determine the class distribution of criminal and delinquent behavior.'" American Sociological Review 47: 433-435.

INCIARDI, J. A. (1978) "The Uniform Crime Reports: some considerations on their shortcomings and utility." Public Data Use 6: 3-16.

International Association of Chiefs of Police [IACP] (1929) Uniform Crime Reporting. New York: author.

JACOB, H. (1975) "Crimes, victims and statistics: some words of caution." Northwestern University. (unpublished)

KALISH, C. B. (1974) Crimes and Victims: A Report on the Dayton-San Jose Pilot Survey of Victimization. National Criminal Justice Information and Statistics Service. Washington, DC: U.S. Government Printing Office.

KITSUSE, J. I. and A. V. CICOUREL (1963) "A note on the uses of official statistics." Social Problems 11: 131-139.

KLECK, G. (1982) "On the use of self-report data to determine the class distribution of criminal and delinquent behavior." American Sociological Review 47: 427-433.

LEHNEN, R. G. and A. J. REISS, Jr. (1978) "Some response effects in the National Crime Survey." Victimology 3: 110-124.

LEHNEN, R. G. and W. G. SKOGAN [eds.] (1981) The National Crime Survey Working Papers. Vol. I: Current and Historical Perspectives. Washington, DC: U.S. Government Printing Office.

LEVINE, J. P. (1978) "Reply to Singer." Criminology 16: 103-107.

——— (1976) "The potential for crime overreporting in criminal victimization surveys." Criminology 14: 307-330.

LOFTIN, C. and R. H. HILL (1974) "Regional subculture and homicide: an examination of the Gastil-Hackney thesis." American Sociological Review 39: 714-724.

MALTZ, M. D. (1977) "Crime statistics in historical perspective." Crime and Delinquency 23: 32-40.

MAXFIELD, M. G., D. A. LEWIS, and R. SZOC (1980) "Producing official crimes: verified crime reports as measures of police output." Social Science Quarterly 61: 221-236.

McCLEARY, R., B. C. NIENSTEDT, and J. M. ERVEN (1982) "Uniform Crime Reports as organizational outcomes: three times series experiments." Social Problems 29: 361-372.

McDONALD, L. (1969) Social Class and Delinquency. London: Farber & Farber.

MESSNER, S. F. (1984) "The 'dark figure' and composite indices of crime: some empirical explorations of alternative data sources." Journal of Criminal Justice 12: 435-444.

MURPHY, L. R. and C. D. COWAN (1976) "Effects of bounding on telescoping in the National Crime Survey." Presented at the Annual Meeting of the American Statistical Association, Boston.

——— and R. W. DODGE (1981) "The Baltimore recall study," pp. 16-21 in R. G. Lehnen and W. G. Skogan (eds.) The National Crime Survey: Working Papers. Vol. I: Current and Historical Perspectives. Washington, DC: U.S. Government Printing Office.

NELSON, J. F. (1979) "Implications for the ecological study of crime: a research note," pp. 21-28 in W. H. Parsonage (ed.) Perspectives on Victimology. Beverly Hills, CA: Sage.

——— (1978) "Alternative measures of crime: a comparison of the Uniform Crime Report and the National Crime Survey in 26 American cities." Presented at the American Society of Criminology meeting in Dallas.

NYE, F. I. (1958) Family Relationships and Delinquent Behavior. New York: John Wiley.

O'BRIEN, R. M. (1983) "Metropolitan structure and violent crime: which measure of crime?" American Sociological Review 48: 434-437.

————D. SHICHOR, and D. L. DECKER (1982) "Urban structure and household victimization of the elderly." International Journal of Aging and Human Development 15: 41-49.

————(1980) "An empirical comparison of the validity of UCR and NCS crime rates." Sociological Quarterly 21: 301-401.

PENICK, B.K.E. and M.E.B. OWENS, III [eds.] (1976) Surveying Crime. Washington, DC: National Academy of Sciences.

PEPINSKY, H. E. (1976) "Police patrolmen's offense reporting behavior." Journal of Research in Crime and Delinquency 13: 33-47.

PETERSILIA, J. (1978) "The validity of criminality data derived from personal interviews," in C. Wellfard (ed.) Quantitative Studies in Criminology. Beverly Hills, CA: Sage.

PITTMAN, D. J. and W. HANDY (1964) "Patterns in criminal aggravated assault." Journal of Criminal Law, Criminology, and Police Science 55: 462-470.

POKORNY, A. D. (1965) "A comparison of homicides in two cities." Journal of Criminal Law, Criminology, and Police Science 56: 479-487.

PORTERFIELD, A. (1946) Youth in Trouble. Fort Worth, TX: Leo Potisham Foundation.

REISS, A. J., Jr. (1978) Final Report for Analytical Studies of Victimization by Crime Using National Crime Survey Panel Data. New Haven, CT: Yale University, Institute for Policy Studies.

————(1967) Studies in Crime and Law Enforcement in Major Metropolitan Areas: Vol. I. Presidents Commission on Law Enforcement and Administration of Justice. Field Surveys III. Washington, DC: U.S. Government Printing Office.

————and A. L. RHODES (1961) "The distribution of juvenile delinquency in the social class structure." American Sociological Review 26: 720-732.

RONCEK, D. W. (1975) "Density and crime: a methodological critique." American Behavioral Scientist 18: 843-860.

ROSSI, P., E. WAITE, C. E. BOSE, and R. E. BERK (1974) "The seriousness of crimes: normative structure and individual differences." American Sociological Review 39: 224-237.

SCHNEIDER, A. L. (1977) The Portland Forward Records Check of Crime Victims: Final Report. Eugene, OR: Institute for Policy Analysis.

SCHUESSLER, K. (1962) "Components of variation in city crime rates." Social Problems 9: 314-323.

SEIDMAN, D. and M. COUZENS (1974) "Getting the crime rate down: political pressure and crime reporting." Law and Society Review 8: 457-493.

SELKE, W. L. and H. E. PEPINSKY (1982) "The politics of police reporting in Indianapolis, 1948-1978." Law and Human Behavior 6: 327-342.

SELLIN, T. (1931) "The bias of a crime index." Journal of the American Institute of Criminal Law and Criminology 22: 335-356.

SHAPLAND, J. M. (1978) "Self-report delinquency in boys ages 11 to 14." British Journal of Criminology 18: 255-266.

SHAW, C. R. and H. D. McKAY (1969) Delinquency Areas. Chicago: University of Chicago Press.

SHELEY, J. F. and J. J. HANLON (1978) "Unintended effects of police decisions to actively enforce laws: implications for the analysis of crime trends." Contemporary Crisis 2: 265-275.

SHERMAN, L. W. (1980) "Causes of police behavior: the current stage of quantitative research." Journal of Research in Crime and Delinquency 17: 69-100.

SHORT, J. F. and F. I. NYE (1958) "Extent of unrecorded juvenile delinquency: tentative conclusions." Journal of Criminal Law and Criminology 49: 296-302.

——(1957) "Reported behavior as a criterion of deviant behavior." Social Problems 5: 207-213.

SINGER, S. A. (1978) "A comment on alleged overreporting." Criminology 16: 99-102.

SKOGAN, W. G. (1984) "Reporting crimes to the police: the status of world research." Journal of Research in Crime and Delinquency 21: 113-137.

——(1981) Issues in the Measurement of Victimization. Washington, DC: U.S. Government Printing Office.

——(1978) Victimization Surveys and Criminal Justice Planning. Law Enforcement Assistance Administration. Washington, DC: U.S. Government Printing Office.

——(1976)."Crime and crime rates," in W. G. Skogan (ed.) Sample Surveys of Victims of Crime. Cambridge, MA: Ballinger.

SMITH, D. A. and C. A. VISHER (1982) "Street-level justice: situational determinants of police arrest decisions." Social Problems 29: 167-177.

SPARKS, R. F. (1981) "Surveys of victimization—an optimistic assessment." Crime and Justice: An Annual Review of Research 3: 1-60.

TITTLE, C. R. and W. J. VILLEMEZ (1977) "Social class and criminality." Social Forces 56: 474-502.

——and D. A. SMITH (1982) "One step forward, two steps back: more on the class/community controversy." American Sociological Review 47: 435-438.

——(1978) "The myth of social class and criminality: an empirical assessment of the empirical evidence." American Sociological Review 43: 643-656.

TOBY, J. (1960) "Review of family relationships and delinquent behavior." American Sociological Review 25: 282-283.

TUCHFARBER, A. and W. R. KLECKA (1976) Random Digit Dialing: Lowering the Cost of Victimization Surveys. Washington, DC: Police Foundation.

TURNER, A. G. (1977) "An experiment to compare three interview procedures in the National Crime Survey." Washington, DC: Statistical Research Division, U.S. Census Bureau. (memorandum, March)

——(1972) The San Jose Methods Test of Known Crime Victims. National Criminal Justice Information and Statistics Service, Law Enforcement Assistance Administration. Washington, DC: U.S. Government Printing Office.

U.S. Bureau of the Census (1977) "Estimates of the population of the United States by age, sex, and race: July 1, 1974 to 1976." U.S. Current Population Reports Series P-25, 643. Washington, DC: U.S. Government Printing Office.

——(1970a) "Household survey of victims of crime: second pretest (Baltimore, Maryland)." Washington, DC: Bureau of the Census, Demographic Surveys Division. (mimeo)

——(1970b) "Victim recall pretest (Washington, D.C.) household surveys of victims of crime." Washington, DC: Bureau of the Census, Demographic Surveys Division. (mimeo)

U.S. Department of Justice (1983) Criminal Victimization in the United States: 1973-1981. Washington, DC: U.S. Government Printing Office.

———(1981a) Dictionary of Criminal Justice Data Terminology. Washington, DC: U.S. Government Printing Office.

———(1981b) Measuring Crime: Bureau of Justice Statistics Bulletin. Washington, DC: U.S. Government Printing Office.

———(1980) Crime and Seasonality. National Crime Survey Report, Bureau of Justice Statistics. Washington, DC: U.S. Government Printing Office.

———(1976a) Criminal Victimization Surveys in Chicago, Detroit, Los Angeles, New York, Philadelphia. Washington, DC: U.S. Government Printing Office.

———(1976b) Criminal Victimization in Eight American Cities. Washington, DC: U.S. Government Printing Office.

———(1975) Criminal Victimization Surveys in 13 American Cities. Washington, DC: U.S. Government Printing Office.

VISHER, C. A. (1983) "Gender, police arrest decisions, and notions of chivalry." Criminology 21: 5-28.

VOSS, H. L. (1963) "Ethnic differentials in delinquency in Honolulu." Journal of Criminal Law, Criminology, and Police Science 54: 322-327.

WALDO, G. P. and T. G. CHIRICOS (1972) "Perceived penal sanction and self-report criminality: a neglected approach to deterrence research." Social Problems 19: 522-540.

WALLERSTEIN, J. S. and C. J. WYLE (1947) "Our law-abiding law breakers." Probation 25: 107-112.

WHEELER, S. (1967) "Criminal statistics: a reformulation of the problem." Journal of Criminal Law, Criminology, and Police Science 58: 317-324.

WILLIAMS, J. R. and M. GOLD (1972) "From delinquent behavior to official delinquency." Social Problems 20: 209-229.

WILSON, J. Q. (1978) Varieties of Police Behavior: The Management of Law and Order in Eight Communities. Cambridge, MA: Harvard University Press.

———(1967) "The police and the delinquent in two cities," pp. 9-30 in S. Wheeler and H. M. Hughes (eds.) Controlling Delinquents. New York: John Wiley.

WOLFGANG, M. E. (1958) Patterns in Criminal Homicide. Philadelphia: University of Pennsylvania Press.

WOLTMAN, H. F. and J. M. BUSHERY (1978) "Results of the NCS maximum personal visit-maximum telephone interview experiment." Washington, DC: U.S. Bureau of the Census. (mimeo)

———(1975) "A panel bias study in the National Crime Survey." Proceedings of the Social Statistics Section of the American Statistical Association.

———and L. CARSTENSEN (1975) Recall bias and telescoping in the National Crime Survey. Washington, DC: U.S. Bureau of the Census. (memorandum, September 23).

YOST, L. R. and R. W. DODGE (1970) "Household survey of victims of crime: second pretest—Baltimore, Maryland." Washington, DC: U.S. Bureau of the Census. (memorandum, November 30).

ZEDLEWSKI, E. W. (1983) "Deterrence findings and data sources: a comparison of Uniform Crime Reports and National Crime Surveys." Journal of Research on Crime and Delinquency 20: 262-276.

INDEX

Absolute rates, 84-87, 101-102
Abt Associates, 107
Ageton, S.S., 12, 76, 77, 84, 86, 94, 95, 96, 116
Akers, R.L., 63, 115
Amir, M., 66, 115

Bailar, B.A., 115
Bailey, L., 52, 88, 104, 115
Beattie, R.H., 29, 88, 103, 115
Bell, D., 27, 115
Berger, A.S., 95, 115
Berk, R.E., 119
Biderman, A., 13, 43, 60, 107, 115
Black, D.J., 25, 31, 32, 38, 83, 115
Blau, J.R., 87, 91, 115
Blau, P.M., 87, 91, 115
Block, C.R., 34, 115
Block, R., 26, 34, 115
Booth, A.D., 89, 91, 115
Bose, C., 119
Bounded interview, 42, 51, 52, 84
Braithwaite, J., 76, 115
Bureau of Justice Statistics, 47
Bushery, J.M., 54, 55, 121
Business respondent, 42

Canter, R.J., 116
Carstensen, L., 121
Catlin, G., 56, 115
Chambliss, W.J., 27, 57, 102, 115
Chiricos, T.G., 63, 121
Chivalry hypothesis, 32
Choldin, H.M., 115
Cicourel, A.V., 37, 118

Clarke, J.P., 63, 64, 116
Clearance, 22
    by arrest, 22
    by exceptional means, 22
    rate, 22
Cohen, J., 89, 116
Cohen, L., 93, 116
Comparability of crime data, 82-84
Convergence of measures, 14, 99
Convergence of results
    absolute rates, 84-87, 101-102
    crime trends, 96-98, 106-107
    demographic characteristics (of offenders), 92-96, 105-106
    relative rates of crime (across jurisdictions), 87-92, 102-105
Counting rule for multiple offenses, 18, 19, 22, 45
Couzens, M., 28, 88, 103, 106, 120
Cowan, C.D., 54, 118
Crime definitions
    UCR, 111-113
    NCS, 113-114
Crime index
    part I, 18, 19, 20, 22, 33
    violent crimes, 19, 20, 33
    property crime, 19, 20, 33
Crime known to the police, 19, 21, 22
Crime recording, 27, 28, 29, 30, 31, 32, 33, 37, 38
Crime reporting, 25, 26, 33, 37
Crime trends, 59, 96-98, 106-107
Criminal justice statistics, need for, 9, 10
Criminal justice system bias, 98, 105
Cross jurisdictional comparisons, 102-105, 110

ABOUT THE AUTHOR

ROBERT M. O'BRIEN is Professor and Head of the Department of Sociology at the University of Oregon. He has published in the areas of measurement, criminology, stratification, and decision-making processes in toxic waste management. He is a coauthor of *Urban Structure and Criminal Victimization* (with David Decker and David Shichor) and coeditor of *Controversies in Environmental Policy* (with Sheldon Kamieniecki and Michael Clarke; forthcoming). O'Brien received his Ph.D. in sociology from the University of Wisconsin (Madison) in 1973.